Bell & Cohn's

Handbook

of Grammar, Style, and Usage

Third Edition

James K. Bell
Adrian A. Cohn
College of San Mateo

Macmillan Publishing Co., Inc.

NEW YORK

Collier Macmillan Publishers

LONDON

For Jonathan
and for Sarah

Contents

The Thought-Fox

Ted Hughes

I imagine this midnight moment's forest:
Something else is alive
Besides the clock's loneliness
And this blank page where my fingers move,

Through the window I see no star:
Something more near
Though deeper within darkness
Is entering the loneliness:

Cold, delicately as the dark snow,
A fox's nose touches twig, leaf;
Two eyes serve a movement, that now
And again now, and now, and now

Sets neat prints into the snow
Between trees, and warily a lame
Shadow lags by stump and in hollow
Of a body that is bold to come

Across the clearings, an eye,
A widening deepening greenness,
Brilliantly, concentratedly,
Coming about its own business

Till, with a sudden sharp hot stink of fox
It enters the dark hold of the head.
The window is starless still; the clock ticks,
The page is printed.

Ted Hughes, "The Thought-Fox," *The Hawk in the Rain* (New York: Harper & Row, 1957). Copyright © 1957 by Ted Hughes. Originally appeared in *The New Yorker* and reprinted by permission of Harper & Row, Publishers, Inc.

Preface

To the Student

The first edition of *Bell & Cohn's Handbook* represented an effort to cut through the gloom and verbosity of the larger college handbooks. Too often such books did not clarify matters: they darkened them, leaving our own students more confused and discouraged than ever, and requiring, consequently, more work and encouragement on our part, and manifold apologies. We agreed with Callimachus: "A big book is a great nuisance." And so our book was to be different: plain and witty, or at least light-hearted—and brief.

Students and teachers alike have responded favorably. Thus in the Third Edition of our *Handbook* we have not tried to make a thing shiny new, nor have we changed for the sake of change: we have tried to improve a book that has helped our own students cope with multitudes of writing problems, making a direct, simple, and practical book even more useful.

We have done this in large part by attempting to answer in print questions our students have asked us in class. In a real sense, then, our *Handbook* has become even more a series of conversations—teacher to student, but also writer to writer—on the craft of public prose (as distinguished from less formal prose). We have changed some entries for the sake of clarity, with particular emphasis on recurring difficulties; we have added new entries on the dictionary, outlining, and plagiarism; we have expanded the cross-references designed to help students who want related information or who might be simply browsing. In addition to including a new research paper, we have appended instructions for writing essay examinations, a glossary of grammatical terms, and a section on the format of business and personal letters.

In concept and in practice, then, *Bell & Cohn's Handbook* is a pocket companion to the art of writing. We have tried to clarify and simplify, and if, in the process of doing so, we seem to have made the book strongly prescriptive, that is only because we are too acutely aware of the horde of exceptions to each rule of convention governing correct prose, and in that awareness have eliminated options and exceptions for the sake of the plain and direct answer.

Using this book is simple. Besides the five sections at the back of the text, there is the major portion of the book, the entries.

You can use the entries as you are writing to check on such diverse matters as grammar, punctuation, style, organization, development, and manuscript preparation. Simply look up the appropriate article as you would look up a word in your dictionary.

You can also use this book when you correct and revise your essays after your instructor has marked them. As a general rule, you will find that he or she has marked each mistake with one of the abbreviations or symbols listed inside the covers of the book. Begin by noting the article that the abbreviation or symbol refers to. Next find the article (arranged alphabetically, of course, like the entries in a dictionary) and read it through. As you read, try to locate those parts that apply particularly to the mistakes you have made. Study these parts carefully. Analyze the examples. Then analyze your own mistake—and correct it.

If you use this *Handbook* conscientiously, you should find one day that you can get along quite well without it. That too is part of its purpose.

James K. Bell
Adrian A. Cohn

Abbreviations—Use abbreviations sparingly. Write out most words in full.

Use abbreviations for

1. Common titles followed by proper names:

   Dr. Henry Jekyll

   Mr. Edward Marshall

   Ms. Rosa Arnaz

   St. James

2. Academic degrees:

   Ph.D.

   M.D.

   MBA

3. *Jr.*, *Sr.*, and *Esq.* following proper names:

   Jonathan Edwards, Jr.

Robert E. Baker, Sr.

Ashley Brown, Esq.

4.   The names of certain well-known organizations and institutions (omitting periods and spaces):

OPEC

FBI

HEW

CIA

UNESCO

Note: When first referring to agencies, organizations, and institutions that may be unfamiliar to your reader, write out the full name and include the initials in parentheses after it. Then, in all subsequent references, use the abbreviation.

5.   Selected technical terms, scientific words, and trade names:

mph

rpm

DDT

FM

CBS

OED (Oxford English Dictionary)

6. *Ante meridiem* and *post meridiem:*

6:15 a.m. (or 6:15 A.M.)

7:00 p.m. (or 7:00 P.M.)

7. Before Christ and *anno domini* ("in the year of the Lord"):

500 B.C.

1776 A.D.

July 21, 1984 A.D.

8. Common Latin expressions:

cf. (*confer*, "compare")

e.g. (*exempli gratia*, "for example")

etc. (*et cetera*, "and others," "and so on")

i.e. (*id est*, "that is")

9. The names of states in addresses. When abbreviating the names of states in addresses, use the two-letter abbreviations shown on page 4. Write or type them in capital letters with no spaces between the letters and no period after them.

Alabama	AL	Montana	MT
Alaska	AK	Nebraska	NE
Arizona	AZ	Nevada	NV
Arkansas	AR	New Hampshire	NH
California	CA	New Jersey	NJ
Colorado	CO	New Mexico	NM
Connecticut	CT	New York	NY
Delaware	DE	North Carolina	NC
District of Columbia	DC	North Dakota	ND
Florida	FL	Ohio	OH
Georgia	GA	Oklahoma	OK
Guam	GU	Oregon	OR
Hawaii	HI	Pennsylvania	PA
Idaho	ID	Puerto Rico	PR
Illinois	IL	Rhode Island	RI
Indiana	IN	South Carolina	SC
Iowa	IA	South Dakota	SD
Kansas	KS	Tennessee	TN
Kentucky	KY	Texas	TX
Louisiana	LA	Utah	UT
Maine	ME	Vermont	VT
Maryland	MD	Virginia	VA
Massachusetts	MA	Virgin Islands	VI
Michigan	MI	Washington	WA
Minnesota	MN	West Virginia	WV
Mississippi	MS	Wisconsin	WI
Missouri	MO	Wyoming	WY

Do not abbreviate titles when they are used without names.

ORIGINAL

The Dr. is here.

REVISION

The doctor is here.

Dr. Jekyll is here.

Do not use abbreviations (especially etc.) merely to save time and space.

ORIGINAL

After a long ride on the subway, we finally reached downtown Lon. & went to look for a rest., where we ate steak, etc. It wasn't long before I began to think of my Tums back in the hotel rm.

REVISION

After a long ride on the subway, we finally reached downtown London and went to look for a restaurant, where we ate steak and kidney pie, mashed potatoes, cabbage, and broiled tomatoes. It wasn't long before I began to think of my Tums back in the hotel room.

Adjectives—Use an adjective to modify ("describe" or "limit") a noun or pronoun.

adj

1. Noun

    Violent movies are suddenly very *popular*. (The
    adjectives *violent* and *popular* modify the noun
    movies.)

2. Pronoun

    They are *successful*, some psychologists say, because
    such movies satisfy our need to be hurt. (The adjective
    successful modifies the pronoun *they*.)

Do not use an adverb in place of an adjective to complete a linking verb.

For example, consider the following sentence: "After a
few drinks, she became the life of the party; but the next
morning she felt *badly* and looked *terribly*." Does the
sentence *sound* right to you? Your ear for language should
tell you that *"felt bad"* and *"looked terrible"* are the
natural expressions, all considerations of grammar aside.
But there *is* a grammatical problem here: *felt* and *looked*
are linking verbs; *badly* and *terribly* are adverb forms; and
these forms cannot be used to "complete" linking verbs.
The reason lies in the nature and function of the linking
verb.

Linking verbs join (or "link") nouns or pronouns to the
words that follow the verb. The most common linking
verbs are forms of the verb *to be: am, are, is, was, were,
would be, have been,* etc. Other linking verbs denote

appearance, condition, or sensation: *appear, become, seem, look, feel, smell, sound, taste,* etc. Usually, such verbs present no difficulty:

> The room was *elegant.* (The noun *room* is joined to the predicate adjective *elegant* by the linking verb *was.*)

> The gift seemed *perfect.* (The noun *gift* is joined to the predicate adjective *perfect* by the linking verb *seemed.*)

> The sardines smelled *good,* and they tasted *delicious.* (The noun *sardines* is joined to the predicate adjective *good* by the linking verb *smelled.* The pronoun *they* is joined to the predicate adjective *delicious* by the linking verb *tasted.*)

However, many linking verbs may also function as other types of verbs. Consider, for instance, the uses of *feel:*

1. *Feel* as a linking verb:

> I *felt* wonderful after jogging three miles. (The linking verb *felt* joins the pronoun *I* to the predicate adjective *wonderful.*)

2. *Feel* as a transitive verb (expressing action on a direct object):

> She was the sort of old lady who carefully *felt* every peach in the bin before buying her apple. (The verb *felt* is not a linking verb. It expresses action; it is

modified by the adverb *carefully*; and it takes a direct object, *peach*.)

3. *Feel* as an intransitive verb (expressing action without taking a direct object):

Jonathan *felt* under the table with his bare feet, and some friendly toes tickled his. (The verb *felt* is not a linking verb. It expresses action, and it is modified by the adverbial phrases *under the table with his bare feet*, but it does not have a direct object.)

You must recognize a linking verb, then, by its *function*: it joins a noun or a pronoun to the words that follow. And to complete a linking verb you must not use an adverb in place of an adjective.

ORIGINAL

After a few drinks, she became the life of the party; but the next morning she felt *badly* and looked *terribly*. (The adverb forms should not be used to complete the linking verbs *felt* and *looked*.)

REVISION

After a few drinks, she became the life of the party; but the next morning she felt *bad* and looked *terrible*. (The adjective forms should be used to complete the linking verbs *felt* and *looked*.)

(See **Adverbs.**)

Adverbs—Use an adverb to modify ("describe" or "limit")   **adv**
a verb, an adjective, or another adverb.

1. Verb

    An old woman in gold-lamé stretch pants and
    glittering high heels *suddenly* danced across the
    street, moving to a tune that only she could hear. (The
    adverb *suddenly* modifies the verb *danced*.)

2. Adjective

    Rags is a *very* lovely, *very* gentle puppy. (The adverb
    very modifies the adjectives *lovely* and *gentle*.)

3. Other Adverbs

    He drives *rather* slowly. (The adverb *rather* modifies
    the adverb *slowly*.)

Do not carelessly confuse adjective and adverb forms.

As a general rule, adverbs are formed from adjectives by
the addition of -*ly*. But most grammarians recognize that
there is no clear-cut distinction between adjectives and
adverbs. For instance, the word *well* (the adverb
corresponding to the adjective *good*) may be used as either
an adjective or an adverb, depending on its function and

meaning: "Tom Wolfe writes *well*" (that is, "with skill"); "I am *well* now" (that is, "in good health"). In the first example, *well* is an adverb; in the second, *well* is an adjective. Other adjectives are also used as adverbs without any change at all; among these we may list the words *little, less, least, long, better, best, worse, worst, much, more,* and *enough.* For the grammarian, these words represent only some of the more elementary difficulties that obscure the distinctions between adjectives and adverbs.

Nevertheless, your own errors will probably result from the simple omissions of the *-ly* or from confusion about certain common adjectives and the corresponding adverbs that do not take the *-ly* ending. In all doubtful cases, check your dictionary.

ORIGINAL	REVISION
He plays baseball *real good.*	He plays baseball *really well.*
I spend *considerable* more than I make.	I spend *considerably* more than I make.
She *sure* knows how to paint.	She *certainly* knows how to paint. (The colloquial *sure* is sometimes acceptable—and better, in our opinion, than the stilted *surely. Certainly* is more appropriate than either in most expository writing.)

(See **Adjectives.**)

Agreement/Pronoun-Antecedent—Make each pronoun   **agr/pa**
agree with its antecedent.

A pronoun agrees with its antecedent (the word it refers
back to) in person, number, and gender.

> *I* broke *my* toe playing football. (*My* is first person
> singular; it refers back to *I*.)

> During the break between semesters, *we* went to *our*
> cabin in the Sierras. (*Our* is first person plural; it refers
> back to *we*.)

> *You* should write *your* paper as soon as possible.
> (*Your* is second person; it may be either singular or
> plural. Here it is singular, referring back to *you*, which
> is also singular in this context.)

> *Jack* and *Edith* always picked out the cherries from
> *their* ice cream. (*Their* is third person plural; it refers
> back to *Jack* and *Edith*.)

> The used-car *salesman* swore by *his* mother's love
> that the Edsel was the best car ever made. (*His* is third
> person singular; it refers back to *salesman*.)

> *Martha St. John* sadly sipped *her* Pernod and
> wondered if Paris was all it was supposed to be. (*Her*
> is third person singular; it refers back to *Martha St.
> John*. Obviously, *her* is of female gender, while *his*, of

course, is masculine. Note that pronouns such as *I,
you, we,* and *they* have no gender—that is, they refer
to both sexes, or to either.)

Note Carefully: *In standard public prose do not use a
singular pronoun to refer to a plural antecedent, or a
plural pronoun to refer to a singular antecedent.*
Note in particular that words like *each, every, either,
anybody, anyone, somebody, someone, everyone, neither,
nobody* and *no one* **are always followed by singular
pronouns.**

A special problem, however, is posed by the awareness
of that language which tends to place women in
subordinate positions. Traditionally, it would be quite
correct to use *his* to refer to both men and women, as in
"*Each student* [singular] should pass *his* [masculine
singular] paper forward." It's easier to say, "*Each student*
should pass *their* [plural] paper forward," but the pronoun
does not agree with its singular antecedent. (In some cases
you might use the plural consistently: "*All students*
should pass *their* papers forward.") It is unfortunate that
as of yet there is no widely accepted pronoun that can
stand for both *his* and *her.* Until some new convention
develops, it is perhaps best to use the cumbersome "his or
her" construction, *depending on the circumstances.* As
George Orwell advised, break any of the rules of grammar
and style rather than say something barbarous.

ORIGINAL

Every boy in the whole world loves *their* dog, even if *they* are mangy beasts. (*Every boy* and *dog* are singular; the pronouns that follow should be singular.)

Anyone can make a mistake on *their* income tax return. (*Anyone* is singular; the pronoun that follows *should* be singular, but, as we noted above, the more formal *his* represents gender discrimination.)

REVISION

Every boy in the whole world loves *his* dog, even if *it* is a mangy beast.

(See **Reference.**)

Anyone can make a mistake on *his* income tax return.

OR:

Anyone can make a mistake on *his* or *her* income tax return.

Agreement/Subject-Verb—Make each verb agree with its subject.   **agr/sv**

1.   A singular subject requires a singular verb; a plural subject requires a plural verb:

> Ice *is* usually hard, clear, and cold. (The singular subject *ice* takes the singular verb *is*.)

> Doctors are usually busy, expensive, and out on Wednesdays. (The plural subject *doctors* takes the plural verb *are*.)

Exceptions

(a)   A plural subject that names either an extent or a quantity taken as a unit requires a singular verb.

> Twenty miles *is* a long walk for anyone. (The plural subject *miles*, taken as a unit, requires a singular verb, *is*.)

> Seven dollars *is* too much to pay for this room, in my opinion. (The plural subject *dollars*, taken as a unit, requires a singular verb, *is*.)

(b)   A singular subject that refers to the members of a group requires a plural verb—when the members are considered to be acting individually.

> The class *are* in their seats now. (The singular subject *class* takes the plural verb *are*—and the plural pronoun *their*—because the members are represented as acting individually.)

2.   Two or more subjects joined by *and* usually take a plural verb:

> Lewis Carroll's *Through the Looking Glass* and *Alice in Wonderland* are two of my niece's favorite books.

> Witchcraft, idolatry, and blasphemy *were* capital crimes in the Massachusetts Bay Colony.

Exceptions

(a)   When the subjects joined by *and* refer to the same person, or when they name things thought of as a logical unit, the verb is singular.

> My friend and colleague *is* a bright young man named Jim.

> This bread and cheese *is* a meal in itself.

(b)   When the subjects joined by *and* are preceded by *each* or *every*, the verb is singular.

> Each wheel and each gear *is* inspected by an expert.

3.   Subjects joined by *or, nor, either . . . or, neither . . . nor* may take a singular or plural verb:

(a)   When the subjects are singular, the verb is singular:

> Neither snow, nor rain, nor heat, nor gloom of night *stays [stops]* these couriers from the swift completion of their appointed rounds.

> > —Inscription on the Main Post Office
> > New York City, adapted from Herodotus

(b)   When both subjects are plural, the verb is plural:

> Since neither the administrators nor the students *were* willing to compromise, the love-in became a riot.

(c)   When one subject is singular and the other is plural, the verb agrees with the nearer subject:

Neither the President nor his advisors fully *understand* the problems of the urban poor.

No spices or flavoring *is* used in this recipe.

Neither you nor she *is* entirely wrong.

4.   The indefinite pronouns *each, either, neither, anybody, anyone, everyone, everybody, someone, somebody, no one, nobody,* and *one* always take a singular verb:

Each of them *is* recalling a different aspect of the murder.

Nobody *knows* the trouble I've seen.

5.   The relative pronouns *who, which,* and *that* are singular if the antecedent is singular, and plural if the antecedent is plural:

Cats that *fight* dogs don't live long. (*That* is plural, and it takes a plural verb.)

A cat that *fights* dogs won't live long. (*That* is singular, and it takes a singular verb.)

She is the kind of woman who *breaks* the bank at Monte Carlo. (*Who* is singular, and it takes a singular verb.)

He is a man *who builds* roads and tunnels that *lead*
nowhere. (*Who* is singular and it takes a singular verb.
That is plural, and it takes a plural verb.)

Problems in Subject-Verb Agreement

1.   Do not be confused by words or phrases that separate
the subject from its verb:

ORIGINAL

The *reason* for the impoverished
condition of my finances *are*
rather embarrassing. (The singular
subject, *reason*, should have a
singular verb, *is*, not the plural
verb *are*. *For the impoverished
condition of my finances* merely
modifies the subject without
influencing the verb in any way.)

REVISION

The *reason* for the impoverished
condition of my finances *is* rather
embarrassing.

2.   Do not be confused by sentences beginning *there is* or
there are; in such sentences, the subject with its modifiers,
if any, follows the verb:

ORIGINAL

There *is* a hundred reasons for
trying. (The plural subject,
reasons, requires a plural verb,
are, not the singular verb *is*.)

REVISION

There *are* a hundred reasons for
trying.

3.   Do not be confused by words that are plural in form but singular in meaning—for instance, *civics*, *economics*, *genetics*, *linguistics*, *mathematics*, *news*, *physics*, *semantics*. Such words take a singular verb:

> *Gymnastics helps* build strong bodies ten ways. (The singular subject, *gymnastics*, takes a singular verb, *helps*.)

A few words that are always plural in form may be either singular or plural in meaning, depending on how they are used: *politics* and *statistics*, for instance, are sometimes singular and sometimes plural. Consult a good college desk dictionary to distinguish the various meanings of these words.

ap

Apostrophe—Use apostrophes to show possession; to make plurals of numbers, letters, and symbols; and to show omissions in contracted words or numbers.

1.   *Possession.* Show possession by the addition of an apostrophe or an apostrophe and s. As a general rule, add only an apostrophe if the word already ends in s:

SINGULAR	PLURAL
the *girl's* books	the *girls'* books
the *boy's* shirts	the *boys'* shirts
Mr. *Johnson's* car	the *Johnsons'* cars
the *child's* toys	the *children's* toys

2.   *Plural of numbers.* Form the plural of numbers by the addition of an apostrophe and *s*:

His 7's are hard to read.

Of all his guns, the .45's were the most deadly.

3.   *Plural of letters.* Form the plural of letters by the addition of an apostrophe and *s*:

Dot your *i*'s and cross your *t*'s.

There are two *o*'s in *too.*

4.   *Plural of symbols.* Form the plural of symbols by the addition of an apostrophe and *s*:

The page was covered with + 's, = 's, and $'s.

5.   *Plural of slang used as written words.* Form the plural of slang words by the addition of an apostrophe and *s*:

Her speech is filled with clichés: I heard at least seven *all right's*, five *far out's*, and four *wow's* in the time it

took to walk down the steps and across the main
parking lot.

6. *Contractions.* Form contractions by using an
apostrophe in the place of missing letters or numbers:

Can't you do anything right?

It's not the heat that gets me; it's the humidity.

The '80 election was a disappointment to the
Harrisons.

Do not use apostrophes with the possessive pronouns *his,*
hers, its, ours, yours, theirs, whose.

WRONG	RIGHT
Here's my car, but where's *your's?*	Here's my car, but where's *yours?*

Never use an apostrophe simply to form a plural.

WRONG	RIGHT
The *Mittrick's* live here.	The *Mittricks* live here.

---

aud   **Audience**—Write for a general audience unless otherwise
instructed.

Who reads your papers? You believe with some certainty that your papers are likely to be read only by your instructors, who know what you have read and discussed, what has happened in class, and what the assignment is. Nevertheless, you should write for a *general audience* in most expository papers. The general audience is "out there": *not* your instructors, *not* a fellow student, but someone who might find your paper on a street corner, someone who knows nothing of your classroom work. This particular someone should be thought of as your audience, the *general audience* for whom you are writing. The general audience should be considered informed, literate, and worthy of your respect. The situation is artificial at this point, but remember that in later life, when you write expository prose, you will most likely be writing for a general audience.

Remember, then:

1.   *Orient your audience.* Fill in background information, because you cannot assume that your audience knows anything about your writing assignment. For instance, suppose that you are writing about Hemingway's story "A Clean, Well-Lighted Place." Identify the author and title; briefly sum up the plot; then state your thesis:

> In his story "A Clean, Well-Lighted Place," Ernest Hemingway presents three main characters: an old man who likes to drink late at a cafe, the "clean, well-lighted place"; a younger waiter who is anxious

to get home to his wife; and an older waiter who is in no hurry because he identifies with those who need a light for the night and because he knows he will not sleep until dawn. The story presents the older waiter's deeply moving confrontation with *nada,* the existential Nothingness that characterizes his universe and, by implication, the world in which many men and women live.

2.   *Write in an appropriate style.* For a general audience, you should avoid extremely colloquial prose on the one hand and excessively formal prose on the other. That means, in effect, that you should write *Standard Editorial English* (see **Sentence Structure/Style** and **Usage**). Colloquial prose is characterized by loose sentence structure and word choices more appropriate to speech than to expository writing. Excessively formal prose is marked by disproportionate use of longer, more involved sentences and highly Latinate diction.

---

awk, k   **Awkward Phrasing**—Phrase each sentence as clearly and forcefully as possible. Revise any wording that seems awkward, clumsy, inept, vague, or ambiguous. Use exact words arranged simply and clearly.

ORIGINAL

The conformist type of parent does not delve into the origin on why he should raise a family or see the great value that consummates in raising a family. In his hands he has a child that he can mold the mind to search or let the child be raised in our ethics and mores of society to be mediocre. The asset of having a parent who will encourage a child to think is worth more than 500 parents who are consistently wanting to do the same as his neighbors. (This is confused, ugly, and verbose. The student has an idea but cannot express it: such prose is painful to read and probably more painful to write.)

REVISION

The parent who merely conforms does not see any great value in raising a family. He doesn't realize that he has a *choice:* he can either let his children grow up believing in the traditional mores of our society, or he can mold their minds to search for individual ideas. A parent who can encourage his children to think is worth five hundred parents who consistently want them to do as their neighbors do. (This is simpler and clearer. But because this passage can now be *read*, the student who wrote it should be able to see that he needs to examine his ideas with some care. In sentence one, for instance, he should see that the word *value* demands some explanation. What value? Who receives it—the parent, the children, society in general? Or is *value* perhaps the wrong word here? The answers to these questions should lead to further rewriting and greater clarity.)

Awkward phrasing comes in such bewildering variety that any attempt at classification is simply futile. But we can often show *why* a given phrase is awkward.

1.   A phrase may be awkward because the writer has chosen the wrong word:

ORIGINAL

His most undesirable attribute is that he is *perverted* to killing people, fighting, and other acts of violence. (He may indeed be perverted, but the use of the word in this construction leads to a series of clumsy phrases where three short verbs would serve better.)

REVISION

His most undesirable attribute is that he kills, fights, and commits other violent acts.

2.   A phrase may be awkward because the writer has used indirect, wordy constructions:

ORIGINAL

By "other-directed" *it is meant* not to be bound by habits, traditions, or prejudices. (*"By . . . it is meant"* is an impersonal construction; it forces the writer to use too many words.)

REVISION

Other-directed means "not bound by habits, traditions, or prejudices."

(See **Impersonal Construction.**)

3.   Awkward phrasing may be simply verbal clutter:

ORIGINAL

Unfortunately, any experience I had that was at all useful (in bringing in an income) was in the class of being either nonpaying or highly professional, and things like motorcycle-racing, scuba-diving, or cat-burgling fell into this vast collection. (This writer uses too many words but has a fine sense of humor. He could be saved.)

REVISION

Unfortunately, any useful experience I had was either unsalaried or highly professional, like motorcycle-racing, scuba-diving, or cat-burgling.

What should you do, then, about revising your own awkward phrasing? Our best advice is to use your dictionary, first of all, and to cut out all unnecessary words. *Be clear, simple, and direct.*

(See **Impersonal Construction, Passive Construction, Sentence Structure/Style,** and **Wrong Word.**)

Brackets—Use brackets within a direct quotation to enclose an explanation, a correction, or a comment.

> "Another reason for this exaggerated enthusiasm [for translations] is that our current poets are at a loss as to what to write. Translation is a way to get a poem without having to go into it for yourself."
>
> —Gene Fowler, "The Poet as Translator"
> (*Trace*, No. 12, 1968–69, p. 372)

A special kind of comment usually enclosed in brackets is the editorial remark *sic,* a Latin word meaning "thus." Use *sic,* enclosed in brackets, to indicate that you are reproducing a word or phrase exactly as it was written.

> Professor Fulton must have been flustered on Wednesday, for this is what he wrote on the chalkboard: "Read Lessen [*sic*] 10 for Thrusday [*sic*]."

(See **Parentheses.**)

Capital Letters—Use capital letters where they are required by the conventions of the written language.

Every written language has its own peculiar rules governing the use of capital letters—rules hardened by tradition and not to be broken by logic. The rules for American English are set down here. Unless you are already famous for your iconoclastic style, you would be wise to learn them.

1.   Capitalize proper nouns and proper adjectives (nouns and adjectives that distinguish an individual person, place, or thing from others of the same class):

> The handsome stranger was Clark Kent.
>
> In England, I drank German beer, ate French food, and went to Swedish movies.

2.   Capitalize the names of races, peoples, tribes, and languages:

He's a Cherokee Indian, but he speaks Japanese like a native.

3.   Capitalize the first words of a sentence or an expression standing for a sentence:

Birds do it.

Wow!

4.   Capitalize the first word of each line of traditional verse:

O western wind, when wilt thou blow
      That the small rain down can rain?
Christ, if my love were in my arms
      And I in my bed again!

5.   Capitalize the first word of a direct quotation:

There is an old saying, "The crowd on the boulevard never grows old." For a certain class in this country, Manhattan is the boulevard, and nowhere else will do.

—Blake Fleetwood, "The New Elite
and an Urban Renaissance"
(*The New York Times Magazine*,
January 14, 1979, p. 26)

6.   Capitalize all references to the Deity:

"In the name of the Father, and of the Son, and of the Holy Ghost, amen."

7.   Capitalize days of the week, the names of months, holy days, holidays, and festivals:

On Saturday, December 25, we will celebrate Christmas as usual—with too many toys and too much food.

8.   Capitalize titles when they appear before the name of the bearer:

I debated with President Lincoln and Senator Douglas.

9.   Capitalize the first word—and each of the other words except unemphatic articles, conjunctions, and prepositions—in the titles of plays, magazines, poems, movies, stories, essays, and musical selections. As a general rule, the articles (the words *the, a,* and *an*) are always unemphatic; prepositions and conjunctions fewer than six letters long are usually unemphatic.

After I saw *Much Ado about Nothing,* I went home and read *As You Like It.*

10.   Capitalize North, East, South, and West, and their combined forms (Middle West, Southwest), when they refer to a specific geographic section of the country. (But do not capitalize such words when they refer merely to direction.)

The Southwest is our fastest growing region.

We headed north and then east.

11.   Capitalize brand names and registered trademarks:

She was wearing tight, faded Levi's and drinking a Coke; from her Keds to her Breck-clean hair, she was one hundred percent American.

Avoid unnecessary capitals.

WRONG	RIGHT
I am taking Accounting and Biology.	I am taking accounting and biology.
	I am taking Accounting 1a and Biology 17b.
Of course I love my Mother.	Of course I love my mother.
	Of course I love Mother. (In this sentence *Mother* is a proper noun and should be capitalized.)

(See **Lowercase Letters.**)

---

case   **Case (of pronouns)**—Use the correct case for each pronoun construction.

Case, grammatically, designates the ending of a word, or a new form of a word, used to show how that word is related to other words in context.

Highly inflected languages, like Latin, use cases extensively to show grammatical relationships. For example, "Canis hominem momordit" means "The dog bit the man." But "Canem homo momordit" means "The man bit the dog." In other words, case shows *who* did *what* to *whom*.

In English, fortunately, only pronouns have a complicated system of cases. As a speaker of the language, you *know* all of these cases, so listing them here would be pointless.

Let us concentrate instead on two principles: first, use the *subject case* of pronouns for the subjects of verbs and the complements of linking verbs; second, use the *object case* of pronouns for the objects of verbs and prepositions.

SUBJECT CASE	OBJECT CASE
(*who, whoever*)	(*Whom, whomever*)
Who loves me?	*Whom* do I love?
I know *who* loves me.	I know *whom* I love.
Whoever you love will suffer.	Love *whomever* you want.
I will love *whoever* did it.	I will love *whomever* I find first.
(*Who* is the subject of *loves*; *whoever* is the subject of *did*.)	(*Whom* is the object of *love* in both sentences; *whomever* is the object of *want* in the third sentence, and the object of *find* in the last sentence.)

Exceptions

Idiomatic speech and informal writing allow us great freedom in using the subject case where the object case is formally required.

>   *Who* do you trust?

>   *Who* do you think you're kidding?

are both grammatically incorrect, for example. But in each sentence the use of *whom* would have sounded stilted.

SUBJECT CASE	OBJECT CASE
(*I, we, he/she, they* as subjects)	(*me, us, him/her, them* as objects)
I said, "Hah! You're a dirty old man!"	He gave *us* the raspberries.
She and *I* sat on my roof one night, and *we* talked until the sun came up.	She taught *me* a lesson.
He agrees that the only solution to the problem will be unacceptable to our parents.	I saw *him* with another woman, and if I know *her*, he's in bad trouble.
They stood just outside my window.	Do you see *them*?
(*I, we, he/she,* and *they* all serve as subjects.)	(*Me, Us, him/her,* and *them* all serve as direct objects of verbs.)

SUBJECT CASE

(*I*, *we*, *he/she*, *they* as complements)

It is *I* that I want to talk about.

It was *they* and *we* who lost all our savings.

I thought it was *he* and *she* I saw together.

But it seems to be *they* who should go.

(*I*, *we*, *he*, *she*, and *they* are complements of linking verbs.)

OBJECT CASE

(*me*, *us*, *him/her*, *them* as objects of prepositions)

Do you have a hug for *me*?

In *us* there was perfect harmony; in *them*, none.

Her husband said to *her* and to *him*, "Just what the hell is going on here?"

Then he stepped on *them* both.

(*Me*, *us*, *him*, *her*, and *them* are objects of prepositions.)

Exceptions

Again, speech and informal writing permit us great freedom in the use of personal pronouns. "It is *I*" sounds stilted. Say, "It's me"—and don't feel guilty about using an object case after a linking verb.

Typical Errors in Pronoun Case

ERROR

Claire and *me* went surfing. (*Me* cannot serve as part of the subject of the verb *went*.)

CORRECTION

Claire and *I* went surfing.

ERROR	CORRECTION
The waves were too big for Claire and *I*. (*I* cannot serve as the object of the preposition *for*; do not be confused by the fact that *Claire* is also the object of the preposition.)	The waves were too big for Claire and *me*.
But I was also interested in why the magazine was popular and to *who* it was most appealing. (*Who* cannot serve as the object of the preposition *to*; *whom* therefore is required.)	But I was also interested in why the magazine was popular and to *whom* it was most appealing.
Whomever it was rang twice. (*Whomever* cannot serve as the complement of the linking verb *is*.)	*Whoever* it was rang twice.
Whom shall I say is calling? (*Whom* cannot serve as the subject of *is calling*; do not be confused by the intervening clause *shall I say*.)	*Who* shall I say is calling?
To *we* spectators speed is no longer very important. (*We*, along with *spectators*, is the object of the preposition *to*; hence you must say *us* spectators.)	To *us* spectators speed is no longer very important.

Us boys down at the brewery get all the free beer we can drink. (*Us*, with *boys*, is a subject; hence you must say *we* boys.)

We boys down at the brewery get all the free beer we can drink.

Cliché—Use clichés and other extremely popular and fashionable expressions only when necessary or effective.

cl

A cliché, specifically, is an overused figure of speech: *that's the way the cookie crumbles; dead as a doornail; high as a kite; happy as a lark; cool as a cucumber; a dog-eat-dog world.* Besides such similes and metaphors, however, the term *cliché* also refers to worn and ragged expressions of all sorts, many of which have lost their original meaning; *toe the line*, for example, originally meant to stand with one's toes touching a line as a starting point for a contest, but the phrase is so little understood now that it is often written *tow the line.* (And our students keep telling us it's a *doggy-dog* world.) Hence any extremely popular or fashionable phrase may be considered a cliché: stock expressions ("last but not least"); quotations ("To be or not to be . . ."); foreign expressions (*"bête noire," "c'est la vie," "che sera sera"*); and slogans of the hour and the latest catch-words ("Right on!" "Far out!").

Every writer is tempted by clichés: a ready-made phrase is a ready-made thought. Not thinking eliminates some of the work of writing. Good writers, however, do their own thinking and their own phrasemaking, although at times a cliché *may* be appropriate and effective. For example: "He was as ugly as sin—but just as much fun!"

Be alert to clichés. They stalk you at every twist of the pen. Scratch your head and one pops up. To cure yourself of a habit as nasty (for a writer) as nose-picking, try writing a paragraph packed with clichés like this one:

Why I Want a College Education

In the fast-moving world of today in which we live, the person who wants to go places in a big hurry needs that old sheepskin. Education is important if you're going to get a good job. Once you leave the nest you have to land on your feet and start running just to keep your head above water in the fast-moving world of today. Without a college diploma you will wind up on the streets along with the rest of the unemployed and the economically deprived, since every day it's harder to get a good job without a college education. In this world life is not just a bowl of cherries; it's a dog-eat-dog battle for survival, best person win, winner take all. You've got to get in there and fight, hammer and tongs, tooth and nail, to win out over your worthy opponent. If you need to climb the ladder of success over other people's dead bodies, do it. But you can't sit back and wait for all the goodies to be handed to you on a golden platter—unless you were born with a silver spoon in your mouth. Every individual is in competition with every other individual in our complex, fast-moving world of today, with its rapidly advancing technology. To beat the other person you need a college education. That's why I'm going to college. And may the best person win!

Colon—Use the colon [:], following a main clause, to introduce a list, an explanation, or a formal quotation, and in certain other constructions.

C:

1. List

   All they ever served were beef dishes: beef Wellington, prime rib, beef Stroganoff, New York steak, ground round.

2. Explanation

   I began to doubt Martha's love: surely the arsenic in my coffee was no accident.

3. Formal Quotation

   In Rex Stout's series of mystery stories, Archie Goodwin and Inspector Cramer delight in badgering one another. Here, for instance, Archie has just insulted Cramer:

His face, chronically red, deepened a shade. His broad shoulders stiffened, and the creases spreading from the corners of his gray-blue eyes showed more as the eyelids tightened. Then, deciding I was playing for a blurt, he controlled it. "Do you know," he asked, "whose opinion of you I would like to have? Darwin's. Where were you while evolution was going on?"

Do not use a colon in the middle of a clause; use the colon only at the end of an independent clause.

ORIGINAL

Among the animals that have pouches are: anteaters, kangaroos, koalas, opossums, and wombats. (Here, the colon is used, incorrectly, in the middle of a clause.)

REVISION

Among the animals that have pouches are anteaters, kangaroos, koalas, opossums, and wombats.

The following are among the animals that have pouches: anteaters, kangaroos, koalas, opossums, and wombats.

4.   Use the colon between chapter and verse in references to the Bible:

Genesis 9:3–8

John 3:1–4

5.   Use the colon between hours and minutes in indicating time:

> It is now 4:05 P.M.
>
> I got up at 5:00 A.M.

6.   Use the colon after the salutation in a business letter:

> Dear Ms. Washington:
>
> To whom it may concern:

Always place the colon outside quotation marks:

> In winter, I often think of the last line of Emerson's poem "The Snowstorm": "The frolic architecture of the snow."

Comma—Use a comma where the structure of a sentence demands one.   C

The comma marks a very slight pause in the flow of a sentence. In speech, such a pause usually follows a rise in the pitch of the voice; that is, the voice actually reaches a higher tone just before the pause. Consequently, if you can "hear" your own writing—and if you remember that writing is a reflection of the spoken language—you will be able to use your natural good judgment in placing commas.

You should also consult the following rules.

1.   Use a comma to separate words, phrases, and clauses in a series:

Words

The beach was bright with striped umbrellas, frosty ice chests, multicolored towels, and lobster-red bodies.

Phrases

At the same party, Martha St. John climbed to the top of the stairs, removed her glass eye, jumped for the chandelier, and swung upside down by her legs, while reciting a poem about Tarzan and apes.

Clauses

Then she ran into the bedroom, she threw herself onto the bed, and she burst into tears and choking sobs.

Exception

The final comma is sometimes omitted in a brief, clear series:

His poems are simple, clear and deeply moving.

But the omission is not particularly daring or modern; it obscures the relationship between the spoken sounds and the written words; and it may be confusing. If you want to be clear, courteous, and exact, leave the final comma where it belongs: in the series.

2.   Use a comma to separate coordinate adjectives (adjectives of equal rank and importance):

> a *tender, succulent* steak
>
> a *beautiful, gentle, sweet* child

To apply a simple test for coordinate adjectives, you can change their order and insert the word *and* (as in *a succulent and tender steak*). If the meaning is still clear, the adjectives are coordinate.

When one adjective is considered part of the noun, however, the adjectives are not coordinate and should not be separated by a comma:

> the *good old* days

Old days is a unit. Thus *good* and *old* are not coordinate. If they were, you could reverse the order and insert *and* without twisting the sense of the phrase. But *the good old days* does not mean *the old and good days*.

3.   Use a comma before the conjunction in a compound sentence:

A compound sentence contains two main clauses—by definition, clauses that *could* stand alone as separate sentences. In a compound sentence, such clauses are usually—but not always—joined by a coordinating conjunction; a semicolon sometimes takes the place of the conjunction:

> Jean raced for the bathroom, *but* I ran for the front door.
> Jean raced for the bathroom; I ran for the front door.

The coordinating conjunctions in English are *and*, *or*, *nor*, *but*, *yet*, and *for*. Note that in the following compound sentences, commas are used before each of these conjunctions:

> Medical researchers have already created a vast variety of mood-controlling drugs, *and* even pills to increase intelligence seem to be within the realm of possibility.

> You must get here on time, *or* you'll miss your plane.

I seldom drink to excess, *nor* do I use tobacco.

"Candy is dandy, *but* liquor is quicker."

He loves fishing, *yet* he seldom has time for it.

No decision was necessary, *for* she left him without a word.

Exception

For a sharper break between the two clauses, a semicolon may be used even when the conjunction is retained:

He said no; *and* that was that.

Caution: Do not confuse a compound sentence with a simple sentence containing a compound predicate—that is, a sentence containing a single subject but two or more verbs. Such a sentence should not have a comma before the conjunction.

ORIGINAL	REVISION
The sun dropped slowly over the horizon, and fell into the sea. (The comma is not required because this is a simple sentence, containing a single subject with two verbs.)	The sun dropped slowly over the horizon and fell into the sea.

4.   Use commas to set off a nonrestrictive word, phrase, or clause following a noun:

Nonrestrictive words, phrases, or clauses simply add more information. They are not essential to the meaning of the sentence—and could be dropped without changing the basic meaning.

   Note how the comma is used with each of the following nonrestrictive constructions. Note, in addition, that the comma also *follows* the word, phrase, or clause when the construction is set in the middle of the sentence:

Word

Roz Throckmorton, *politician*, will speak in the park tonight.

Ernst, *my neighbor*, shoots pool and drinks bourbon almost every night.

Phrase

The sky, *darkening suddenly*, seemed to be afloat in scudding black clouds.

My money, *not being essential to her happiness*, surely was not a factor in her falling in love with me, was it?

Clause

I was very embarrassed when my date, *who was only slightly drunk*, broke a heel and went crashing halfway down the stairs, as her glass hit the ceiling and a shower of champagne fell on the other guests.

Wilma Hunt, *who happens to be a great disco dancer,* is my best friend.

5.   Use a comma to set off a long introductory phrase or a subordinate clause:

Phrase

After waiting in the bar for two hours, we were hungry enough to eat braised buffalo liver au gratin.

On the night of the big game, twelve people turned out to welcome the team home.

Clause

Although he was perhaps America's greatest poet, Ezra Pound still spent twelve years in a federal insane asylum awaiting trial for treason allegedly committed during World War II.

While walking on the beach one day, I found a walrus eating oysters. [An *elliptical* clause: the subject and part of the verb—"I was"—are understood even though not directly expressed.]

6.   Use a comma to set off a nonrestrictive subordinate clause at the end of a sentence; omit the comma if the clause is restrictive:

Nonrestrictive

I won't marry him, *even though he is young and handsome.*

I wanted that antique very much, *although I knew I could not afford it.*

Restrictive

I wouldn't marry him *if he had a million dollars.*

I learned my lesson *after I found out my antique was a reproduction.*

7.   Use a comma after an introductory participial or gerund construction:

Participles are verbal adjectives. The present participle ends in -*ing*; the past participle ends in -*ed* when the verb is regular, but in irregular verbs its ending varies according to the custom of the language. Thus *walking* and *swimming* are forms of the present participle; *walked* and *swum* are forms of the past participle.

Gerunds are verbal *nouns*. Like present participles, gerunds end in -*ing*. To tell the difference between a gerund and a present participle, simply decide whether the word functions as a noun or an adjective. Unless you are especially interested in grammar, however, you probably will feel no compelling drive to discern the difference. Don't worry about it: the distinction is usually unimportant when it comes to this rule of comma punctuation.

Participial Constructions

Grabbing my can of insect-killer, I quickly annihilated a silverfish. (*Grabbing* is a present participle.)

Having driven for ten hours, she could no longer feel her big toe. (*Having driven* is a past participle.)

Gerund Constructions

By killing just one silverfish, I benefit humanity and myself, perpetually at war with the insect population. (*Killing* is a gerund.)

After driving all those hours, Dipsy learned she was going in the wrong direction. (*Driving* is a gerund.)

8.   A word, phrase, or clause that interrupts the sentence in any way should usually be set off by commas:

Word

And that, *my love,* is the story of my life.

It is, *however,* very difficult to hit a silverfish from more than ten feet away.

Phrase

That song, *in my opinion,* is silly and unimaginative.

Mike would be much improved, *on the contrary*, by a sudden impact with a moving train.

Clause

Dipsy's map, *it seems to me*, bears closer scrutiny.

The lights down below, *she thought*, are very beautiful at this time of morning, when the sun is just beginning to rise out of the darkness and into layers of purple and pink sky.

9.   Use a comma to separate a brief direct quotation from the rest of the sentence:

Jonathan Wild looked closely at her and said, "I think I could learn to like you."

"In fact," he added, "you're the most beautiful golden retriever I've ever seen."

10.   Use a comma to set off words and phrases that mark a transition in thought at the beginning of a sentence:

However, he knew that Martha would never let him keep a dog.

Indeed, Martha hated dogs.

On the other hand, Martha was something of a beast herself, and. . . .

After all, a dog that beautiful would undoubtedly behave better than Martha, who insisted on taking out her glass eye at the most inappropriate moments and polishing it on her sleeve like a piece of costume jewelry.

11.   Use a comma to set off numbers indicating thousands:

10,000 $5,230,000

12.   Use a comma to separate day and year in writing dates:

Today is March 5, 1981.

On July 30, 1975, I left for London.

Note: It is not necessary to use a comma when only the month and year are given: "August 1980 was a happy month for me."

13.   Use commas with geographical names and addresses:

I arrived in Krailling, Germany, after traveling from London.

The raid was made at 419 Via Maria, Santa Barbara, California.

14.   Use a comma to prevent confusion:

For Carlotta, Agnes was a faithful friend and a charming companion.

Just before, I had run into the rear bumper of a
Redwood City police car.

What will be, will be.

15.   Always place the comma inside the quotation marks,
unless the quotation itself is followed by a parenthesis:

I have just finished reading "Flight," which is one of
my favorite short stories.

I have just finished reading "Flight" (you know, by
John Steinbeck), which is one of my favorite short
stories.

Despite this profusion of rules, we have severely *limited*
our account of the circumstances under which commas
should be used. We should now repeat a point we made
earlier: check the rules when you need to, but, for the most
part, *rely on your common sense:* an inner ear will usually
tell you when to use commas.

CS

Comma Splice—Do not write two main clauses joined by
a comma.

This construction—a "comma splice"—is a gross
mechanical error, in the minds of many instructors,

because it suggests that the writer is unable to recognize basic sentence units. In other words, joining two complete sentences with *just* a comma is a violation of sacred rules, although many professional writers do it. It is a good idea, nevertheless, to break rules only when you can get away with doing so—in this case, outside the classroom, in fiction, poetry, letters, and in informal writing generally.

1.   Correct some comma splices by using a coordinating conjunction with the comma:

COMMA SPLICE

He has completed his research, he will report his findings to the class today.

CORRECTION

He has completed his research, *and* he will report his findings to the class today.

(See **Comma.**)

2.   Correct some comma splices by replacing the comma with a semicolon:

He has completed his research; he will report his findings to the class today.

(See **Semicolon.**)

3.   Correct some comma splices by replacing the comma with a period:

He has completed his research. He will report his findings to the class today.

4.   Correct some comma splices by using a dash:

COMMA SPLICE

I like Julian Symon's novels, he always tells an exciting story.

CORRECTION

I like Julian Symon's novels—he always tells an exciting story.

(See **Dash.**)

5.   Correct some comma splices by using a colon:

COMMA SPLICE

Everyone should have a telephone with an on-off switch, it gives him a tie with the outside world but allows him his privacy, too.

CORRECTION

Everyone should have a telephone with an on-off switch: it gives him a tie with the outside world but allows him his privacy, too.

(See **Colon.**)

Note: Many comma splices result from elementary confusion about a class of words called *conjunctive adverbs*. These are words and phrases which, like conjunctions, *link* ideas but technically serve as *adverbs* (hence their name). Conjunctive adverbs in English include such terms as *then, first, second, however, nevertheless, for example, nonetheless, finally, furthermore, likewise, moreover, meanwhile, soon, hence,*

accordingly, therefore, thus, then, and *consequently.*
While the list is by no means complete, it does suggest
some of the qualities of conjunctive adverbs: they link
ideas together, they show relationships, they indicate
comparison and contrast, they signal how one thing
happens after or as a result of another thing: that is, they
function as *directional signs* in English. *But they cannot
be used to join clauses grammatically, as in the following
comma-spliced sentences:*

Ken wanted to go to the World Series, *however* he
couldn't get tickets.

That model airplane is very realistic looking, *for
example* notice the detail on the wings.

Citizen Kane was an innovative movie, *thus* it has
been shown in many film classes, *therefore* thousands
of students have had an opportunity to study it.

We drove seven hours to reach the mountains, *then* we
spent the rest of the day skiing.

I tried and tried to fix my car, *finally* I called a garage.

Such sentences can be repaired in any of the ways listed
above, or you may want to completely rewrite the
sentence. Consider these corrections, for instance:

Semicolon

Ken wanted to go to the World Series; *however,* he
couldn't get tickets.

That model airplane is very realistic looking; *for example*, notice the detail on the wings.

Colon plus conjunction

Citizen Kane was an innovative movie: *thus* it has been shown in many film classes, *and therefore* thousands of students have had an opportunity to study it.

Period

We drove several hours to reach the mountains. *Then* we spent the rest of the day skiing.

Conjunction

I tried and tried to fix my car, *but finally* I called a garage.

The method you choose will depend on the sentences themselves and their context. If you have just written a short sentence, you may now want a longer one; if you have just written a long sentence, you may now want two shorter ones. You may want the unique rhythm—the half-break in the flow of a sentence—created by a semicolon. Don't correct the error mechanically: correct it with a sense of style.

Conclusion—Conclude your essays; don't just stop   **conc**
writing them.

Use the conclusion as a convenient exit for both reader
and writer, a way of stepping graciously out the door. The
conclusion gives you a chance to draw inferences, assert
the importance of your ideas, or summarize your basic
points. Use that chance.

1.   Concluding the paragraph:

Most paragraphs used as parts of essays have no
"concluding" sentence. The reason for this is, of course,
that these paragraphs lead on to something else in
the essay. But the paragraph written as a short
composition—the kind of paragraph you often write in
college—usually does have a sentence that we can label
"conclusion." There are no simple rules for such a
sentence; you will have to be guided by your own good
sense. We will simply remind you that at the end of any
composition you have your final chance to impress your
reader. Even in writing a "one-paragraph essay" you will
probably want to use this opportunity. To do so, *end with
a sentence that restates your main idea or draws a logical
conclusion from the evidence you have presented.*
    Consider one example of the effective conclusion in the
paragraph. Here, Vance Packard begins with the following

topic sentence: "The early nineteen fifties witnessed the beginnings of a revolution in American advertising: Madison Avenue became conscious of the *unconscious*." In the concluding sentence he cleverly rephrases this idea by substituting *ad* for Madison Avenue and *id* (the source of our unconscious desires) for the *unconscious:* "The ad is being tailored to meet the needs of the id."

The early nineteen fifties witnessed the beginning of a revolution in American advertising: Madison Avenue became conscious of the *unconscious.* Evidence had piled up that the responses of consumers to the questions of market researchers were frequently unreliable—in other words, that people often don't want what they say they want. Some years ago, for instance, a great automobile company committed one of the costliest blunders in automobile history through reliance on old-style "nose counting" methods. Direct consumer surveys indicated that people wanted a sensible car in tune with the times—without frills, maneuverable and easy to park. A glance at today's cars—elongated, fish-finned and in riotous technicolor—shows how misleading were the results of the survey. Errors of this sort convinced manufacturers and advertisers that they must take into account the irrationality of consumer behavior—that they must carry their surveys into the

submerged areas of the human mind. The result is a
strange and rather exotic phenomenon entirely new
to the market place—the use of a kind of mass
psychoanalysis to guide campaigns of persuasion. The
ad is being tailored to meet the needs of the id.

> —Vance Packard, "The Ad and the Id"
> (*Harper's Bazaar*, August 1967, p. 97)

2.   Concluding the essay:

The last paragraph of your essay should drive home your
main points by summarizing or repeating your thesis. *And
under no circumstances should you introduce a new idea
in the last paragraph*, for, naturally, your reader would
expect further development of such a point.

To get into the final paragraph, use appropriate
transitional words: *then, finally, thus, in short, therefore*
(but not *in conclusion*, which should be reserved for
longer works). For instance, in the following paragraph,
George C. McGhee concludes his comments on the lost art
of conversation by writing:

And finally, I want to encourage the pixie of the
conversation who can add zest and interest. Our talk
too often reflects the dull things we do all day.
Conversation does not always have to be earnest.
Provocation, whimsy, laughter, mockery, and

> flirtation all have their place in the art of good
> conversation, of which has been said, "Be prompt
> without being stubborn, refute without argument,
> clothe weighty matters in a motley garb."
>
> —George C. McGhee, "The Lost Art of
> Conversation" (*Saturday Review*, 1975)

While we recommend, and some instructors require, a transitional expression early in the final paragraph of expository essays written for college classes, the professional may use subtler devices, while *implying* a transitional word. For instance, here is the final paragraph from Patricia Cross's "The Education of Women Today and Tomorrow." Her thesis is that education and women's rights will profoundly concern both men and women in the new world of tomorrow.

> Both men and women have a stake in that new world.
> While women may be more motivated and sensitive to
> changing sex roles, the education of women is a task
> that must be understood and shared by everyone. Let
> us be firm in our resolve to provide educational
> opportunity to all, but let us use strength wherever we
> find it—in men and women, young and old, rich and
> poor, black and white, those who question and hold
> back as well as those who are impatient and rush

ahead. Women's rights is no more a woman's issue
than civil rights is a minority issue. The future belongs
to all of us, and if we don't make it better, who will?

> —K. Patricia Cross, "The Education of
> Women Today and Tomorrow,"
> *The American Woman: Who Will She Be?*
> by McBee and Blake (Encino, Ca.: Glencoe, 1974)

Finally, here is a concluding paragraph from Robert
Benchley's "Throwing Back the European Offensive." His
transitional phrase, *whichever way*, refers back to the two
methods he has recommended to combat the menace of
returning travelers.

> Whichever way you pick to defend yourself against
> the assaults of people who want to tell you about
> Europe, don't forget that it was I who told you how.
> I'm going to Europe myself next year and if you try to
> pull either of these systems on *me* when I get back, I
> will recognize them at once, and it will just go all the
> harder with you. But of course, *I* will have something
> to tell that will be worth hearing.

> —*The Early Worm* (New York:
> Harper & Row, 1927)

con

Continuity—Write so that your ideas flow logically from sentence to sentence and from paragraph to paragraph—that is, give your writing continuity.

Continuity literally means "holding together." It's what gives your writing a sense of smoothness as you go from one idea to the next. You get continuity *first* by good organization, because the clear, logical arrangement makes the order of thought easy to follow.

(See **Organization.**)

You get continuity *second* from the language you use to tell your reader how your ideas fit together—you get it in transitions (connecting words and phrases).

(See **Transitions.**)

Dangling Modifiers—Do not write sentences containing dangling modifiers.

Modifiers—almost always verbal phrases, in this case—are said to "dangle" when they fail to relate sensibly to the subject of the sentence: that is, they fail to modify the noun or pronoun that immediately follows the phrase, so that the sense of the sentence goes askew. For example, one student writes, *"Besides lying on the beach, my time will be occupied in other constructive ways."* Now, that sentence *says,* "My time was lying on the beach." Obviously the logic is twisted. The student *means,* "I will be lying on the beach"; hence he should have written, *"Besides lying on the beach,* I will spend my time in other constructive ways." Now the modifier no longer dangles. It hangs there just where it belongs: in front of the word *I.*

1.   Correct some dangling modifiers by changing the main clause so that the modifier does, in fact, modify the subject.

DANGLING MODIFIER	CORRECTION

Washing the car, his legs got splattered with mud. (His legs washed the car?)

Washing the car, he splattered his legs with mud.

With bags of groceries in their arms, the dogs knocked over the children. (The dogs were carrying groceries?)

With bags of groceries in their arms, the children were knocked over by the dogs.

2.   Correct some dangling modifiers by expanding the phrase into a subordinate clause:

DANGLING MODIFIER	CORRECTION

While typing, my dog began to lick my toes. (The dog was *typing*, too?)

While I was typing, my dog began to lick my toes.

Flying at 20,000 feet, the cars looked like toys. (The cars were flying maybe, but not at 20,000 feet.)

When we were flying at 20,000 feet, the cars looked like toys.

To dance well, a sense of rhythm is necessary. (A sense of rhythm dances?)

If you want to dance well, you need a sense of rhythm.

Dash—Use a dash (typed as two unspaced hyphens) to set   **d--**
off a sharp turn of thought within the sentence; to
emphasize a parenthetical expression; and to set off
parenthetical or appositional material introduced by
certain expressions.

1.   To set off a sharp turn of thought within the sentence:

I kissed her passionately and found—good
grief!—that none of her teeth were hers.

2.   To emphasize a parenthetical expression:

Early morning—just as the birds waken and the black
night turns dark shades of purple—is my favorite time
of all.

3.   To set off parenthetical or appositional material
introduced by certain expressions (*namely, for example,
that is, for instance,* etc.):

Only two things in life are inevitable—*namely,* death
and taxes.

Right now his romantic life is extremely
complicated—*that is,* he has two dates for Saturday
night.

Some movie stars are also political activists—*for
example,* Jane Fonda.

Note: Dashes emphasize; parentheses deemphasize; commas simply enclose. Use dashes discreetly.

Note also that dashes always go outside quotation marks:

> Whitman's "O' Captain, My Captain"—Jeb's favorite poem—is about Abraham Lincoln.

---

dev

Development—Develop each paragraph fully and completely.

Except for a few extremely brief paragraphs, used mainly for transition or for emphasis of a significant point, each paragraph should be developed in adequate detail. The following *methods of development* are most commonly used.

1.   Develop some paragraphs by descriptive details:

> It was amusing to look around the *filthy little scullery* and think that only a *double door* was between us and the *dining-room.* There sat the *customers* in all their splendour—*spotless tablecloths, bowls of flowers, mirrors,* and *gilt cornices* and *painted cherubim;* and here, just a *few feet away,* we in our *disgusting filth. For it really was disgusting filth.* There was no time to

sweep the *floor* till evening, and we slithered about in
a compound of *soapy water, lettuce-leaves, torn paper*
and *trampled food.* A *dozen waiters* with their *coats*
off, showing their *sweaty armpits,* sat at the *table*
mixing *salads* and sticking *their thumbs* into the
cream pots. The *room* had a *dirty, mixed smell* of *food*
and *sweat.* Everywhere in the *cupboards,* behind the
piles of *crockery,* were *squalid stores* of *food* that the
waiters had stolen. There were only *two sinks,* and *no
washing basin,* and it was nothing unusual for a
waiter to wash his *face* in the *water* in which *clean
crockery* was rinsing. But the *customers* saw nothing
of this. There were a *coco-nut mat* and a *mirror*
outside the *dining-room door,* and the *waiters* used to
preen themselves and go in looking the *picture* of
cleanliness.

> —George Orwell, *Down and Out in Paris and
> London* (New York: Pocket Books, 1954, p. 78)

Edmund Morris also uses vivid descriptive technique
in the following paragraph about our twenty-sixth
President. Morris' writing, like Orwell's, is so graphic one
can almost see the figure he describes:

The nerves that link all this mass of muscle are
abnormally active. Roosevelt is not a twitcher—in
moments of repose he is almost cataleptically
still—but when talking his entire body mimes the

rapidity of his thoughts. The right hand shoots out, bunches into a fist, and smacks into the left palm; the heels click together, the neck bulls forward; then, in a spasm of amusement, his face contorts, his head tosses back, spectacle-ribbon flying, and he shakes from head to foot with laughter. A moment later he is listening with passionate concentration, crouching forward and massaging the speaker's shoulder as if to wring more information out of him. Should he hear something not to his liking, he recoils as if stung, and the blood rushes to his face.

—Edmund Morris, *The Rise of Theodore Roosevelt*
(New York: Coward, McCann & Geoghegan, 1979, p. 21)

2. Develop some paragraphs by facts and statistics:

The events of which I write must have occurred somewhat more than 2 billion years ago. As nearly as science can tell that is the approximate age of the earth, and the ocean must be very nearly as old. It is possible now to discover the age of the rocks that compose the crust of the earth by measuring the rate of decay of the radioactive materials they contain. The oldest rocks found anywhere on earth—in Manitoba—are about 2.3 billion years old. Allowing 100 million years or so for the cooling of the earth's crust, we arrive at the supposition that the tempestuous and violent events connected with our planet's birth occurred nearly 2½ billion years ago.

But this is only a minimum estimate, for rocks
indicating an even greater age may be found any time.

—Rachel Carson, *The Sea Around Us*
(New York: Oxford University Press, 1950, p. 4)

3. Develop some paragraphs by multiple examples:

Many of the costs at a fine restaurant are in the
overhead department. Ambrosia's yearly payroll is
$500,000, including $40,000 for the *chef d' cuisine*.
The long-stemmed roses that adorn each table cost an
average of $1,800 a month and the bud vases they are
put in cost $28 each. A Royal Copenhagen *demi-tasse*
and saucer are another $28 each. The special glasses
Ambrosia buys for its rare wines cost $30 each. The
restaurant gets a better break on other glassware, with
champagne glasses billed at $32 a dozen. But
replacement costs for all items are fierce. Ambrosia
has to replace silver every 10 to 14 months, glassware
every four to six months and china every six to eight
months.

—Thomas M. Self, "Ambrosia's Geril and
Gosta Muller" (*Executive*, July 1979, p. 22)

4. Develop some paragraphs by an extended example:

The most elementary example of the unforeseeable
effects of technical progress is furnished by drugs.

You have a cold in the head; you take an aspirin. The headache disappears, but aspirin has other actions besides doing away with headaches. In the beginning we were really oblivious of these side effects; but, I should imagine, by now everyone has read articles warning against the use of aspirin because of its possible effects, say, on the blood picture. Grave hemorrhages have appeared in people who habitually took two or three aspirins daily. Yet aspirin was thought the perfect remedy a scant ten years ago—on the ground that no side effects were to be feared. Now such effects begin to appear in what was, and is, probably the most harmless of all drugs.

—Jacques Ellul, "Technological Progress Is Always Ambiguous" (John Wilkinson, trans., *Technology and Culture*, Fall 1962)

5.   Develop some paragraphs by an anecdote—that is, by a story told to illustrate your point:

There is a need for simple personal communication. Certainly teachers must protect themselves from the cannibalism of the young that would eat their hearts out; but caution can go so far that academic life becomes frigid. For instance, recently at Hamilton there was a hassle between administration and faculty, and many students were indignant because they thought good teachers were treated shabbily. Learning about it from the students, I brought it up

with some of the teachers. They were astounded that
the students knew; they were deeply touched that
they cared. "If I had known that was how they felt,"
said one teacher wistfully, "I should have made a
different decision and fought it out."

—Paul Goodman, "Crisis and the New Spirit,"
Utopian Essays and Practical Proposals
(New York: Random House, 1962)

6.   Develop some paragraphs by hypothetical
illustration—that is, by examples or stories invented to
illustrate your ideas:

An egghead is anyone who seems to be so absorbed in
the pursuit of knowledge that he hardly sees the
obvious pleasures of life—"partying" three times a
week, "getting wasted" on Saturday night, and lying to
your parents about your reasons for staggering home at
three in the morning when curfew is at twelve sharp.
Instead of living, the egghead thinks. For example,
consider Jonathan Square. Does he ever date girls, go
to dances, watch television, or listen to "together"
music? The answer is definitely "No!" When I see him
in the hall each morning, his head is bent, his feet
shuffle lethargically, his back twists into a question
mark above the twelve books under his right arm;
his appearance unequivocally suggests lofty
contemplation. At noon, while everyone else gossips

and giggles, Jon Square sits silently in a corner, thumbing the worn pages of a massive philosophy text; from time to time, his eyes glaze over like a lizard's. And what he does in the evening is no secret to anyone; while Mozart tinkles away, or Beethoven blares, Jonathan Square nods and dreams over his books or reflects on the human condition and the sadness of the world without joy.

7. Develop some paragraphs by analogy—that is, by an extended point-by-point comparison:

They made a robot in the shape of a dragonfly and named it Ranger VII, thereby expressing their hope that it would range the face of the moon. For eyes, they gave it camera lenses, and taught it how to photograph by blinking the shutters. Near the place where its nose should have been, they put a radio antenna like a saucer, and taught the robot how to send pictures back through the saucer to earth. When all this was done, they folded the dragonfly's wings, set the mechanical insect on top of a rocket, and fired the rocket into orbit around the earth. Finally they shot the robot out of the orbit, told it to unfold its wings, and pointed it onto a curving path across 243,665 miles of sky. The path ended in a dry lunar lakebed that hadn't been thought important enough to be named.

—John Lear, "What the Moon Ranger Couldn't See" (*Saturday Review*, September 5, 1964, p. 35)

8. Develop some paragraphs by definition:

A word's context is its setting, the way it fits in with the other words and phrases around it. Context analysis, then, is figuring out what a word means by seeing how it fits in with the other words and phrases around it.

—Kathryn A. Blake, *College Reading Skills*
(Englewood Cliffs, N.J.: Prentice Hall, 1973, p. 297)

9. Develop some paragraphs by an appeal to authority—that is, by quoting and paraphrasing a reliable source:

Although some wine drinkers think it's sacrilegious to add anything to champagne, it's used in a number of very popular drinks. One of the best known is the Mimosa—equal parts of champagne and orange juice. I'm not alone in preferring it to any other mixed drink: This is a favorite of Michael Broadbent, director of Christie's wine department in London, who confesses that he actually prefers Bucks Fizz (as this drink is called in England) to plain champagne "unless the champagne is well aged." He adds, "I'm afraid I have lush tastes." And Robert Meyzen of La Caravelle points out that "it's full of vitamins and easy on the liver." The trick to making this drink, which is particularly enjoyable with brunch, is to use freshly squeezed orange juice.

—Alexis Bespaloff, "Cool and Composed: Beguiling Summer Wine Drinks," (*New York*, July 23, 1979, p. 66)

10.   Develop some paragraphs by a combination of methods:

Today no one bestrides our narrow world like a colossus; we have no giants who play roles which one can imagine no one else playing in their stead. There are a few figures on the margin of uniqueness, perhaps: Adenauer, Nehru, Tito, De Gaulle, Chiang Kai-shek, Mao Tse-tung. But there seems to be none in the epic style of those mighty figures of our recent past who seized history with both hands and gave it an imprint, even a direction, which it otherwise might not have had. As De Gaulle himself remarked on hearing of Stalin's death, "The age of giants is over." Whatever one thought, whether one admired or detested Roosevelt or Churchill, Stalin or Hitler, one nevertheless felt the sheer weight of such personalities on one's existence. We feel no comparable pressures today. Our own President, with all his pleasant qualities, has more or less explicitly renounced any desire to impress his own views on history. The Macmillans, Khrushchevs and Gronchis have measurably less specific gravity than their predecessors. Other men could be in their places as leaders of America or Britain or Russia or Italy without any change in the course of history. Why ours should thus be an age without heroes, and whether

this condition is good or bad for us and for
civilization, are topics worthy of investigation.

—Arthur M. Schlesinger, Jr.,
"The Decline of Greatness"
(*The Saturday Evening Post*,
November 1, 1958, p. 25)

Dialogue: Problems in Punctuation—In writing dialogue, **dia**
observe the conventions of punctuation and paragraphing.

1.   Use a comma with the verb of saying:

Martha said, "It's time for tea."

"It's time for tea," Martha said.

2.   Use a question mark or exclamation point if the
dialogue requires it:

Martha asked, "Are you ready for tea?"

"Are you ready for tea?" Martha asked.

Martha exclaimed, "Nuts to tea!"

"Nuts to tea!" Martha exclaimed.

3.   When the verb of saying interrupts a complete sentence, set off the verb with commas:

> "You know," Martha said, "I'd rather have gin than tea."

4.   When the verb of saying ends a complete sentence and is followed by a new sentence spoken by the same person, (a) place a period after the verb and (b) begin the new sentence with a quotation mark and a capital letter:

> "Let me make you a martini," Martha said. "How much vermouth do you take?"

5.   Since written dialogue represents the speech of two or more persons, conventions require that you begin a new paragraph with each new speaker, no matter how short his or her bit of dialogue. Brief passages of description and narrative are usually included as part of the new paragraph:

> "My name is Martha."
> "Do you always drink martinis?" he asked.
> She said, "Of course."
> "Perhaps, just once, I could make a Manhattan for you," he said. "Would you like that?"
> "I'd like that very much," Martha replied, shaking her hair back out of her eyes. "Do you make Manhattans for every girl you meet?"

Bradford smiled. "No," he said, "I sometimes make stingers."

His friend James Barton interrupted, looking up over his cup of coffee. "For some girls, he only opens a can of beer."

(See **Quotation Marks.**)

Dictionary—Consult a good dictionary to answer any questions you have about words—their spelling, pronunciation, derivation, meanings, and use.

dcty

Although dictionaries date back at least as far as the fifteenth century, the first to gain wide recognition in the English-speaking world was a dictionary written by one man—Dr. Samuel Johnson. Published in 1755, Johnson's dictionary had taken eight years to compile and was more than 2,000 pages long. Several years later, Noah Webster, realizing that American English was becoming markedly different from British English, spent twenty years writing a dictionary with some 70,000 entries.

Today dictionaries are available in wide variety, ranging from paperback pocket versions to multivolume tomes complete with magnifying glass. The one-man producer has given way to teams of researchers and editors whose task it is to keep up with the new words and changing meanings that form our language.

The most practical dictionary for the student is probably an abridged desk—or collegiate—dictionary. In addition to their main section of 200,000 to 500,000 vocabulary entries, these dictionaries include much other helpful information, from lists of abbreviations, biographical names, and place names, to punctuation, spelling, and colleges and universities in the United States.

After you have reviewed the table of contents, be sure to read the instructions for the use of your dictionary. A check of the preface and explanatory notes will tell you, for example, whether the first or the last definition of a word is the most current or common one, and it will list and explain the various parts of the vocabulary entries.

Order of Vocabulary Entries

All words defined in any dictionary are always given in alphabetical order. At the top of each page are two *guide words* to help you find entries quickly. The left-hand guide word is the first word on the page, and the right-hand one is the last word on the page. All other words on the page appear alphabetically between these two words.

Content of Vocabulary Entries

Although dictionaries differ somewhat in the kinds of information given for each word, almost all contain the following elements.

ENTRY WORD

Printed in boldface type, this gives the correct spelling and where applicable an alternate spelling. It also shows how the word is divided into syllables.

PRONUNCIATION

Pronunciation is usually set off in parentheses following the entry word. A key to the pronunciation symbols is given in the front of the dictionary and often at the bottom of every other page. For words of two or more syllables, a stress mark (') appears directly before or after the syllable that receives the strongest emphasis.

PARTS OF SPEECH

Parts of speech are abbreviated (n. for noun, etc.) and help you identify the way a word functions. Many words are used as more than one part of speech. To find the meaning you are looking for, first check the part of speech in the entry.

WORD ORIGIN

The origin and development of a word—its *etymology*—
are shown by earlier forms of the word in English
and, usually, other languages. The etymology may use
special symbols or abbreviations, such as < or *f.*, meaning
"derived from."

DEFINITIONS

All of the word's definitions are listed. Some dictionaries
give the earliest meaning first, while others give the most
current or common meaning first. Check the preface and
instructions at the beginning of the dictionary to see
which method it follows. Many dictionaries also include
in the definition a phrase or sentence to show how the
word is used in context, in actual speech or writing.

SYNONYMS

Many dictionaries list words with nearly the same
meaning. These words, called *synonyms*, usually appear
directly after the definition.

Use your dictionary when the need arises, and you will
find it the most valuable "textbook" you have ever owned.
(With the possible exception, of course, of the one you
now hold in your hand.)

Division (of words into syllables)—When the last word of a line must be continued on the next line, divide the word only between syllables.

As a general rule, divide as seldom as possible. Never divide the last word on a page, and never divide a one-syllable word. Always check the syllabification of a word in your dictionary: you *cannot* rely on guesswork.

ORIGINAL

Vincent van Gogh's *Sun-flowers* is the most wid-ely reproduced painting of all time, I have be-en told.
(*Widely* can only be divided after the *e*. *Been* cannot be divided because it has only one syllable.)

REVISION

Vincent van Gogh's *Sun-flowers* is the most wide-ly reproduced painting of all time, I have been told.
(*Sunflowers* and *widely* are divided properly between syllables. *Been* is not divided.)

div

Ellipsis—Use ellipsis marks (three periods) to show omissions from quoted material.

ORIGINAL

He was talented, this child with the golden voice, and he knew it.

"Classification is closely related to analysis; in fact, it is sometimes seen as an aspect of the same mental process. But there is a difference."

ELLIPTICAL TEXT

He was talented . . . and he knew it. (Ellipsis marks used in place of omitted material.)

"Classification is closely related to analysis. . . . But there is a difference." (Note that when the ellipsis comes at the end of a sentence, you must also add a period, making a total of *four* "periods.")

Use a full line of spaced periods to indicate omission of an entire paragraph or one or more entire lines of poetry.

ORIGINAL	ELLIPTICAL TEXT
Whenas in silks my Julia goes,	Whenas in silks my Julia goes,

Then, then, methinks how sweetly
    flows
	Then, then, methinks how sweetly
	    flows

The liquefaction of her clothes.	The liquefaction of her clothes.
Next, when I cast mine eyes and see	....
That brave vibration each way free,	Oh, how that glittering taketh me!
Oh, how that glittering taketh me!	

—Robert Herrick,
"Upon Julia's Clothes"

Exclamation Point—Use the exclamation point (!) after an
emphatic word, phrase, or clause.

ex

Word

"Stop!"
"Damn!"

Phrase

"What a beautiful day!"

Clause

"It *can't* be empty!"

Place the exclamation point inside quotation marks when it is part of the quoted material; otherwise, place it outside:

The captain shouted, "All hands on deck!"

Look at those "creeps"!

Do not use a period or a comma with an exclamation point:

ORIGINAL

"Get away from there!," he shouted.

REVISION

"Get away from there!" he shouted.

In standard expository prose, do not use more than one exclamation point at a time:

ORIGINAL

"Don't go near the water!!!!" Gatsby yelled to the woman in the fur coat.

REVISION

"Don't go near the water!" Gatsby yelled to the woman in the fur coat.

Do not use an exclamation mark for a mild command:

ORIGINAL

Try not to be late for dinner, dear!

REVISION

Try not to be late for dinner, dear.

Fragmentary Sentence—Do not write grammatically incomplete sentences.

To do so may appear to be a crime against common sense and good manners, especially in writing formal expository prose, where the writer is required to demonstrate a command of grammar, style, and sentence structure in *every* sentence.

Of course, almost everyone writes occasional sentence fragments—perhaps influenced by the current language of advertising, in which fragments are rife. Many professional writers of fiction and nonfiction also use fragments freely and effectively, but we do not regard such constructions as fragments; instead, we call them *virtual sentences* because, in context, they have the force and effect of complete sentences.

What knowledgeable writers do instinctively and well, however, students writers may do badly, out of ignorance and inexperience. Our advice, then, is to avoid sentence fragments altogether, especially in expository writing, unless you can justify each of them in a footnote.

The following *types* of sentence fragments occur frequently:

1. Subordinate clauses punctuated as complete sentences:

Subordinate clauses are clauses introduced by subordinate conjunctions—words such as *if, after, before, because, since, when, although, though, while, whenever,* and *whereas.* Even though such a clause has, by definition, both a subject and a verb, it does not express a complete thought and should not be punctuated as a complete sentence.

ORIGINAL	REVISION
Lefty asked her to come. *Whenever she could.*	Lefty asked her to come *whenever she could.*
Please pass the parsnips. *If it's not too much trouble.*	Please pass the parsnips, *if it's not too much trouble.*

2. Verbal phrases punctuated as complete sentences:

ORIGINAL	REVISION
Tom, *working hard on his book.* (This verbal phrase cannot stand alone as a sentence. Either the phrase must be changed to a	Tom, *working hard on his book, failed to remember his wedding anniversary.*

clause or something else must be added to make the sentence complete.)

OR:

Tom *was working hard on his book.*

Even as it is, newspapers no longer seem very profitable. *Witnessed by the fact that in many large cities, the dailies have had to consolidate to survive as one instead of dying as two or more.*

Even as it is, newspapers no longer seem very profitable, *witnessed by the fact that in many large cities, the dailies have had to consolidate to survive as one instead of dying as two or more.*

Each week many violent shows blaze across the television screen. *Adding color and variety to the dull lives of the masses.*

Each week many violent shows blaze across the television screen, *adding color and variety to the dull lives of the masses.* (The error is corrected in these last two examples by joining the sentence fragment to the preceding sentence, where it properly belongs. But both fragments seemed to occur because the writers wanted to emphasize the idea contained in the phrase. Hence, although their grammar was incorrect, their motives were pure.)

3.   Appositives (nouns or noun substitutes) punctuated as complete sentences:

ORIGINAL	REVISION
At the sound of the bell, she emerged from her daydream. *A dream as beautiful as anything she had ever known.* (The appositive, improperly punctuated as a complete sentence, is grammatically a part of the preceding sentence.)	At the sound of the bell, she emerged from her daydream—*a dream as beautiful as anything she had ever known.* (The dash emphasizes the idea contained in the fragment and makes the fragment part of the preceding sentence.)
Americans, in their never-ending race with success, have created an economic system which has only served to further enslave them in the materialistic life. *A life based on greed, guilt, exploitation, and hate.* (This very emphatic statement *should* be set off—by a dash.)	Americans, in their never-ending race with success, have created an economic system which has only served to further enslave them in the materialistic life—*a life based on greed, guilt, exploitation, and hate.* (Now the appositive is an emphatic part of the preceding sentence.)

4.   Part of a compound predicate punctuated as a complete sentence when it should be an integral part of the preceding sentence:

ORIGINAL	REVISION
Good service is too often ignored. *And is too seldom rewarded.*	Good service is too often ignored *and is too seldom rewarded.*

The man from the telephone company installed my phone. *And then stayed for a martini.* (In both examples, the second sentence is simply part of a compound predicate that belongs, grammatically, to the preceding sentence.)

The man from the telephone company installed my phone *and then stayed for a martini.*

Hyphen—Hyphenate the last word in a line where necessary; hyphenate certain compound words; use hyphens for clarity.

1.   Hyphenate the last word in a line where necessary (see **Division**):

From their report, he sensed that the members of the entertainment committee were ignorant of the club's actual fiscal condition.

Note: Divide words only at syllables. Do not divide a word without first checking its syllabification in your dictionary.

2.   Hyphenate certain compound words:

(a)   Use a hyphen before the suffix *-elect:*

president-elect

bride-elect

(b) Use a hyphen after the prefixes *ex-*, *self-*, and *all-:*

ex-president

self-defeating

all-inclusive

(c) Use a hyphen after a prefix that precedes a proper noun:

pro-American

post-Vatican II

pre-World War II

(d) Use a hyphen after a prefix ending in *i-* or *a-* when the root word begins with the same letter:

semi-independent

extra-atmospheric

(e) Hyphenate compound adjectives which immediately precede a noun:

He gained a hard-won victory.

I left on a well-earned vacation.

This is take-a-good-friend-to-lunch week.

Note: Compound adjectives that occur after the noun generally are not hyphenated:

My vacation was *well earned*.

His victory was *hard won*.

(f)   Hyphenate numbers twenty-one to ninety-nine wherever they occur:

She acted as if she were twenty-one, but she looked as if she were sixty-five.

(g)   Hyphenate certain compound nouns:

mother-in-law; has-been; editor-in-chief

Since rules governing the use of hyphens with compound nouns vary with time and usage, you should consult your dictionary when writing virtually any of them.

3.   Hyphenate for clarity:

To get her mind off that horrible day, she sought a new form of *recreation*.

As part of the centennial celebration, the town's citizens attempted a *re-creation* of the famous Battle of Groaning Board that took place there in 1881.

He wore his light blue suit. (The suit is light in weight and blue in color.)

He wore his light-blue suit. (The suit's color is a light blue.)

Impersonal Construction—Avoid impersonal constructions wherever possible.

Impersonal constructions are not *bad*: they are *weak*; they lack force; they soften your prose. These consequences result from the nature of the impersonal construction: it is a subject-verb combination in which the subject refers to nothing definite and the verb expresses little or no *action*. For example, "*It was believed* that the student rebellion was a communist plot." The pronoun *it* has no antecedent; *believed* expresses a state of mind. "*There are* hordes of people milling around the accident." In this sentence, the expletive *there* displaces the subject (*hordes*) and forces a flabby verb (*are*) into the sentence. Far better to say, "I believe the student rebellion was a communist plot." Or, "Hordes of people mill around the accident."

Note, however, that the very nature of the language requires *some* impersonal constructions: "*It seems* cold in here." "*It is* snowing."

Nevertheless, you should try to change every impersonal construction to more forceful, more direct constructions, as in the following examples:

ORIGINAL	REVISION
It was very crowded: *there were* a lot of people at the party.	A lot of people came to the party: people sat in every chair and stood and chatted in the middle of the room.
It seemed to me that every time I turned around, *there was* somebody asking for another drink.	Every time I turned around, someone was asking for another drink.

---

intro   **Introduction**—The first paragraph of an essay should try to do two things: (1) interest the reader; (2) state the thesis.

The basic technique is simple: don't begin by taking two steps backward; instead, dive into your subject. In doing so, you can catch the attention of your reader in many ways, a few of which we will comment on here. When you have your reader "hooked," state your thesis immediately—at the end of the first paragraph, if possible.

Narrative Introductions

The narrative introduction begins with a brief story; it shows people *acting,* as in this opening paragraph from an essay on college students during the Great Depression of the 1930s. The thesis is stated at the beginning of the second paragraph:

> Across the campus of Oklahoma A. and M. College moved a weird procession. At the front was an ancient open flivver sufficiently battered to be termed "collegiate." In its front seat were two boys; in its back seat a bale of hay. There followed another car, differing from the first only in the number and kind of dents in its fenders and body. It was also manned by two boys. Its back seat was occupied by a large crate of protesting poultry. Then came a fifth boy leading a Jersey cow. The cow refused to be influenced by the obvious impatience of the motorized portion of the procession, so it was hours later when the strange group finally arrived in front of a house on the outskirts of the college town. The poultry was given a back yard coop in which to live and, presumably, to lay eggs. The cow was tethered in an adjoining field. Then from some recesses in the battered hulls of the flivvers the boys pulled out some 200 quarts of canned fruits and vegetables and a dozen cured hams. With meat and vegetables in the cellar and prospective eggs

and milk in the back yard, the five were ready for
higher education.

*College students have probably developed more
ingenious ways of beating the depression than any
other group in America.*

—Gilbert Love, "College Students Are
Beating the Depression" (*School and
Society*, XXXVIII, June 10, 1933)

Or look at this narrative opening: it uses a brief,
humorous incident to set the stage for the thesis statement
at the end of the second paragraph. (Actually, the concept
is one paragraph; the paragraph division occurs because of
the dialogue.)

On vacation in rural New England, the president of an
Eastern university woke up one night with sharp
abdominal pains. He got to the nearest hospital, where
a local technician took a sample of his blood and
confirmed the doctor's verdict: appendicitis.
Everything was being readied for the operation, when
the surgeon learned that the patient, like himself, was
a Rotarian. At this news he paused.

"Better do that blood test again," he said
thoughtfully. "The lab girl isn't very good." A fresh
sample was taken, and this time the white count
proved normal. His appendix in fine shape—he had
nothing more than indigestion—the educator left the

hospital with his faith in Rotarians unshaken. *But he vowed never again to place blind trust in a medical laboratory.*

—Maya Pines, "Danger in Our Medical Labs"
(*Harper's Magazine*, October 1963, p. 84)

Expository Introductions

The expository opening begins by explaining or describing. Sometimes the expository opening paragraph begins with a thesis statement, as in this paragraph from "Pit Barbecue for a Hungry Crowd":

Cooking underground is an ancient art. Here in the West it was initiated by the Indians, who discovered that deer and buffalo tasted mighty good when steam-cooked in an earth-covered pit. Later cattle ranchers and cowboys out on the range adopted the idea for their beef suppers.

—*Sunset*, August 1979, p. 78

Sometimes the expository introduction is a carefully detailed description:

The artist, David Hockney, wears a white shirt with a faint double brown stripe, sleeves half rolled up; a bright-red loose-weave straight-bottomed tie; black trousers, with broad gray vertical stripes, that are held up by yellow braces (the fly flap at the top unbuttoned and some red and gray paint spots here and there); no shoes; and one green sock and one brown sock (the green sock has a hole in the toe). He will shortly don a white floppy cotton cap with a peak that looks like the sort of thing worn by French golfers at the turn of the century. *He is forty at this point, and gives little sign of realizing that he is a man walking a tight-rope between once upon a time and happily ever after.*

—"Profiles" (*The New Yorker,*
July 30, 1979, p. 35)

Another way to get the interest of your reader in an expository introduction is to begin with a direct quotation—sometimes from a literary source, sometimes from a central figure expressing an important idea or attitude in your essay. Look at the next paragraph, for example: a direct quotation introduces the subject and at the same time leads to the thesis statement in the last sentence in the paragraph.

"It's not my fault! Nothing in this lousy world is my fault, don't you see that? I don't want it to be and it can't be and it won't be." This outcry comes from Kerouac's Sal Paradise, but it expresses the deep conviction of multitudes of irresponsibles in the age of self-pity. *It is a curious paradox that, while the self is the center of all things, the self is never to blame for anything.*

> —Robert Elliot Fitch, "The Irresponsibles,"
> *Odyssey of the Self-Centered Self* (New York:
> Harcourt Brace Jovanovich, 1960, 1961)

Finally, we come to the type of expository opening paragraph that gets interest by presenting facts and figures of a rather startling nature, as in this opening paragraph:

> Over one million Americans have already been slaughtered in highway accidents. A million more will be killed over the next 15 years. *Irate safety experts say that fully two-thirds of all traffic victims could be spared their lives if auto manufacturers could place less emphasis on "styling" and more on "crash-worthiness."*

> —Ralph Ginzburg, "S.O.B. Detroit"
> (*Fact*, May–June 1964)

In brief, the good introduction, like a short skirt or a flashy car, gets attention: it says, "Look!" But it does more than that, of course—for it also leads to the thesis statement, often the last sentence of the first paragraph or the first sentence of the second paragraph; and on your thesis statement hangs all the rest of the essay.

ital

Italics—Use italics (underlining, in handwritten and typed manuscripts) for certain titles, words and expressions, letters, numbers, and names.

1.   Use italics for the titles of newspapers, magazines, pamphlets, books, paintings, sculptures, plays, films, television shows, and musical productions.

NEWSPAPERS

the New York *Times* (or the *New York Times*)

the San Francisco *Examiner* (or the *San Francisco Examiner*)

MAGAZINES

National Geographic

Time

PAMPHLETS

Tom Paine's *Common Sense*

BOOKS

War and Peace

Rhetoric in a Modern Mode

PAINTINGS AND SCULPTURE

> Leonardo's *Mona Lisa*
> Rembrandt's *The Night Watch*
> Michelangelo's *David*

PLAYS

> Shaw's *Pygmalion*
> Shakespeare's *Romeo and Juliet*

FILMS

> Harold Lloyd's *The Freshman*
> *Kramer vs. Kramer*

TELEVISION SHOWS

> *Wide World of Sports*
> *Sesame Street*

MUSICAL PRODUCTIONS

> *Oklahoma!*
> *Evita*
> Verdi's *Il Trovatore*

Note: Use quotation marks, not italics, for the titles of unpublished manuscripts, book chapters, short stories, reviews, articles, songs, and brief poems. (See **Quotation Marks.**)

2. Use italics for words, letters, numbers, and symbols used as such:

WORDS

His sentences suffer from too many *and*'s.

LETTERS

The *e* in *come* is silent.

Students frequently leave out the *o* in *environment*.

NUMBERS

Her *3*'s and *8*'s look very much alike.

SYMBOLS

To get the area of a circle, use the formula πr^2.

Avoid the use of *&* in place of *and*.

3. Use italics for foreign words or expressions not yet anglicized:

bête noire

che sera

sic

4.   Use italics to emphasize certain words and expressions:

> "Guess what? I have a date with *her*!"

> "How *could* you?"

5.   Use italics for the names of ships, trains, and airplanes:

> The *Queen Mary* is docked permanently in Long Beach.

> The *Orient Express* is now history.

> Miraculously no one was injured when Japan Air Line's DC-8 *Shiga* accidentally landed in San Francisco Bay.

Logic—In writing anything, use clear, careful logic and sound common sense.

If a passage is marked *Logic?* in one of your essays, your instructor means that what you have written is not reasoned: it lacks real thought, convincing evidence of good judgment, persuasive deductions. The question *Logic?* really means "*Think!*"

You should, however, be able to recognize certain logical fallacies that you might conceivably commit and will certainly come across in your everyday reading of magazines, newspapers, letters, even textbooks. Such fallacies crop up with even greater frequency—and greater immunity—in conversation, all the more reason to know them by name. Hence you should learn to recognize and analyze the following common logical fallacies: *abstractions; appeal to emotions; causation; false analogy; hasty generalization; name-calling; non sequiturs; undefined terms;* and *unqualified generalizations.*

1.   Abstractions

Abstract words describe qualities common to a *group* of things—*beauty, truth, difficulty*. They also name spiritual, intellectual, and emotional states—*honesty, immorality, fear*. Such words are absolutely necessary to all thought and writing, certainly; but be wary. Some abstract words are like bear traps. Concealed by the tangle of language, they lie hidden, ready to grab and cripple you. *Communism, Americanism, welfare state, racism*—when you get carelessly close to these words, your writing is in real danger, because you are walking in a field laden with emotional snares. *The American way of life*, you feel, is an extraordinarily good thing; we agree. But *don't* write about it as though it were real, like a car, which you can get into, drive away, and park under a full moon. *It is an abstraction.* Treat it as such. Acknowledge that millions of Americans share it—but millions of others don't. And how much of it and what each group shares and means by it differs from individual to individual, and the differences change almost hourly. Thus you must not write, "The American way of life is threatened by the international communist conspiracy, which hopes to exploit the growing racism of our welfare state in order to destroy Americanism completely." *Logic?* What do those words *mean?* Where did you get these ideas? How can you prove them? In other words, you're being excessively emotional, and your emotions have whirled you into a logical vacuum where *words* have become *things.* Beware the abstraction.

2.   Appeal to Emotions

In expository and argumentative writing, it is unfair to appeal strongly to your reader's emotions: you sway his judgment by twisting his feelings. Thus in arguing about capital punishment, you should avoid the temptation to tell your reader in gruesome detail exactly how the condemned man suffers, or how, because of his childhood, he couldn't help himself. "His father, an alcoholic, beat him without mercy; his mother, a full-time slut and a part-time prostitute, let him go hungry all day long, his diapers unchanged for days, when he was only two years old. Does this man deserve to die, even though he tortured four people to death?"

Maybe not, but that's no argument against capital punishment: it's an attempt to make us feel sorry for a particular murderer and thereby make us condemn a legal procedure. It is good rhetorical strategy, perhaps, but a critical reader will spot it—and condemn it—for what it is: a logically unjustified appeal to our emotions.

3.   Causation

The fallacy of causation is known in logic as the *post hoc, ergo propter hoc* fallacy. The Latin means, "After this, therefore because of this." That is, it designates the

fallacious belief that one event *necessarily* causes another
that follows it. "Jean stopped visiting New York when
the price of gas skyrocketed." Good reasoning?
No—something else might have caused Jean to stop
visiting New York, like too many other activities. More
likely, however, a *combination* of causes brought about
this particular result. Perhaps Jean now prefers to visit
Philadelphia; and perhaps she has a new friend who
prefers to do the driving; perhaps, moreover, all of the
people Jean used to visit in New York have moved. *Any*
number of causes might account for Jean's no longer
visiting New York. It is probably true, in fact, that for
every result there is a complicated set of causes. Certainly
it is *not* true that anything that immediately follows an
event has been *caused* by that event. Beware the fallacy of
causation.

4. False Analogy

Analogy is an extended, point-by-point comparison of two
essentially dissimilar things. It follows therefore that an
analogy can be used *only* to illustrate a point, never to
prove it. In this sense, then, analogies used in
argumentation are *always* false, because they
misleadingly seem to offer the substance of logical
reasoning. For example, let's argue that men are not free to
choose their own destiny, that every event in life is
determined for every individual. We might argue by this
analogy: "Life is like a great chess game. God, or some

other force just as powerful, is playing a kind of game with Himself, using us as pawns, while a special few are knights and bishops, or kings and queens. He moves you one square as he attacks, say, the white queen by putting pressure on one of her bishops. Then he deliberately sacrifices you in order to improve his position. Boooom! You're dead, man, knocked off by the queen's bishop. And what does it all mean? Nothing. It's just a game, an absurd game, and your life is just as absurd and meaningless as mine, or Queen Elizabeth's. Life is a farce."

Now that is an interesting analogy—sophomoric, but interesting. What does it prove? As the man said, "Nothing. It's just a game. . . ." Anybody can make any kind of analogy; but he or she still *proves* nothing, no matter how convincing the analogy sounds. All analogies, therefore, must be used with care—because all analogies are false analogies.

5.   Hasty Generalization

A hasty generalization is a general statement based on too few instances. "My adopted daughter Lisa is very bright and very beautiful. My adopted son Jonathan is a bright and beautiful boy. All adopted children must be bright and beautiful." Not true: some adopted children, like some teachers, must be plain and dull; some adopted children, like some college students, must have average looks and average minds. In fact, as we all know, we can expect infinite variations in adopted children—even in

Jonathan and Lisa, who are probably alike in very few
ways.

Do not try to prove a broad general statement with only
a few instances. (See also *Unqualified Generalizations,*
p. 109.)

6.   Name-calling

Name-calling is a logical fallacy only when you fail to
show that the unfavorable expressions you have applied
to the subject under discussion are accurate, valid
descriptions. "I am a decent, civilized man. But John, who
opposes me, is an arrogant son-of-a-bitch." That's
name-calling—an unfair tactic in argument or debate. On
the other hand, if you can substantiate your accusations,
you are on sounder logical ground. First of all, define your
terms. What is an *arrogant son-of-a-bitch*? Second, show
that John really does have the qualities set forth in your
definition. Then, depending on how sound your
definition is, you may have a valid criticism of John
instead of an emotional, unreasoning condemnation.

7.   Non Sequiturs

Non sequitur, in Latin, means, "It does not follow." Let us
use the term in a very broad sense to designate a
conclusion that does not follow logically from the
evidence on which it is based—usually not evidence at
all, in fact, but a universal generalization accepted

without question. "He must be awfully lazy if he's on welfare." This is a non sequitur because the statement includes the questionable assumption that only *lazy* men and women are on welfare. If you think at all, however, you'll soon realize that this assumption is not fair or valid because many people on welfare are simply unfortunate victims of circumstances: children on welfare, for instance, or men whose crafts have been hit by an economic recession, such as happens periodically in aerospace industries.

Other non sequiturs may be analyzed in the same way: "He's a millionaire, so obviously he's a conservative." "He's not a communist; after all, he attends Mass regularly." "She's only twenty, so she couldn't be the manager." It does not follow that a millionaire is necessarily a conservative. It does not follow that someone who attends Mass regularly is, say, a Democrat instead of a communist. And it does not follow that young people cannot have responsible jobs. Each of these non sequiturs is based on an unquestioned, highly general assumption rather than on logical evidence.

8. Undefined Terms

Often an argument is simply meaningless because the writer has failed to define his terms accurately or at all. Was the war in Vietnam an act of genocide, for instance? Without a full definition of the word *genocide*, we can circle this question as energetically as a dog chases its own tail—with about as much result. Now, *genocide* cooperates: it is an easy word to define. It means, according to *Webster's Third New International Dictionary of the English Language* (Springfield, Massachusetts: G. & C. Merriam Company, Publishers, 1961), "the use of deliberate systematic measures (as killing, bodily or mental injury, unlivable conditions, preventions of births) calculated to bring about the extermination of a racial, political, or cultural group or to destroy the language, religion, or culture of a group." With *evidence* of genocide, one may take the argument from there: at least there would be some point in proceeding.

But other words are much more difficult to pin down. *Americanism? Liberalism?* Do they seem too hard to define? Well, then, take an easy word, like *nice*. We all know what *nice* means, don't we? Yet it has at least fifteen *basic* meanings, according to the *Oxford English Dictionary*. Its early meanings—"foolish, stupid, senseless"; "wanton, loose-mannered, lascivious"—are not so nice at all.

Is he a nice boy—or isn't he? Not even *he* knows for sure.

Nothing can be gained in argumentation without full and accurate definition of important terms.

9. Unqualified Generalizations

A generalization is a broad statement about a number of particulars; a concept or an idea about a group of things drawn from observation of them. Unfortunately, most of the generalizations that sail blithely through our speech and writing are not our own ideas but someone else's, absorbed like oxygen from the atmosphere. The Japanese, for example, believe that Koreans are cruel and Chinese are dirty, stupid, and untrustworthy. The Koreans, on the other hand, hold similar beliefs about the Japanese and Chinese, and the Chinese think of Koreans and Japanese in much the same way.

What we have just said may be partly true. But if you accepted these general statements as *the* truth, then we have hoodwinked you—with a set of *unqualified* generalizations. Some Japanese may be prejudiced against Koreans; *some* Koreans may hate the Chinese; *a few* Chinese may loathe all Koreans, Japanese, Russians, Germans, Blacks, and Jews. But not *all*, certainly, in any of these cases. Hence the generalizations must be *qualified*.

In making general statements, then, use words like *some, many, most, a few, perhaps, maybe, possibly*, and conditional verbs like *may* and *might*. Even so, "we may be tempted to agree with Justice Holmes that 'the chief end of man is to frame general propositions, and no general proposition is worth a damn'" (Lionel Ruby, "Are All Generalizations False?" from *The Art of Making Sense*, Philadelphia: Lippincott, 1954).

Lowercase Letters—Do not use unnecessary capital
letters. Use lowercase letters instead, especially for
common nouns, points of the compass, and certain other
common constructions. (See **Capitalization.**)

lc

1. Common nouns:

   He is a junior in college.

   He plans to major in history.

   Wisconsin in the fall is an explosion of color.

2. Points of the compass:

   He is heading east for his vacation.

   The aircraft headed north, then east, and finally
   settled on a northeasterly course.

3. Family relationships when used with possessive
pronouns:

   Mr. and Mrs. Smith will visit his mother.

   (BUT: We will visit Mother today.)

   Because he needed money, John wrote a long letter to
   his father.

   (BUT: John wrote to Father asking for more money.)

4. Seasons of the year:

You may prefer *fall* and *winter,* but I love *spring* and *summer.*

5. After a colon:

These are not dark days: *these* are great days. . . .

6. After a semicolon:

Simon will go to Chicago; *he* plans to visit with his grandfather.

The books are by the same author; *however,* the quality of the writing is extremely uneven.

7. For the first word after an interrupted quotation:

"We can't go," he said, "*because* tonight we have to study our math."

"I will attend the University of Oslo this summer," he said, "*in* order to learn the Norwegian language."

8. For the first word in a quotation that is not a complete sentence:

He wrote that Wednesday's meeting would be "*one* of the most crucial" in the history of the student body.

This piece of legislation, according to our representatives, "*must* be defeated."

Manuscript Preparation—Prepare your manuscript exactly as directed by your instructor, or follow these generally accepted standards established by the Modern Language Association:

1. Either type your manuscript or use a pen with blue or black ink.

2. *Paper.* Type on one side only of good white paper, 8½ by 11 inches in size. If you do not type, use standard composition paper (notebook paper)—*not paper torn from a spiral binder.*

3. *Typing.* Type with double-spacing throughout, except for long quotations, which should be single-spaced and set off from the body of the manuscript by wider margins. *If you use a pen, skip every other line.*

4. *Margins.* Consistently leave margins of from 1 to 1½ inches at the top, bottom, and sides of each page *except*

the first. The first page is special. On the first page, center the title of your essay about two inches from the top of the page; then start your first line about one inch below the title.

5. *Title page.* Your title page is a cover for your essay. Center your title halfway down the page. In the top right-hand corner, endorse your paper with the following information: your name; the course; the date on which the paper is handed in.

Example: Richard Savage
Communications 11, MFW 2
January 1, 1984

6. *Pagination.* Beginning with page 2, number your pages consecutively throughout the manuscript, placing the number in the right-hand corner at the top of the page.

Note: Your title page, being only a cover, is not counted as part of your manuscript and, of course, is not numbered. Since your first page—which has the title of your essay at the top of the page—is *obviously* your first page, it does not need to have the number 1 written on it. (See **Titles** and the section on **The Research Paper.**

---

mar **Margins**—Leave generous margins—from 1 to 1½ inches—at the top, bottom, and both sides of your paper.

Although a page with generous margins is more attractive than a cramped, crowded page, this rule has little to do with the appearance of your paper; it is designed, instead, to give your instructor sufficient space for comments, questions, and corrections.

While no one expects an even right-hand margin, you can avoid a ragged margin by the judicious use of hyphens. (See **Division** and **Hyphens.**)

Misplaced Modifiers—To say clearly and precisely what you mean, place modifiers as close to the modified words as possible.

mm

A modifier is a word, phrase, or clause that qualifies, limits, or restricts the meaning of another word or phrase. In order to prevent confusion, modifiers must be clearly related to what they modify. When the relationship is not clear, the modifier is misplaced—that is, in the wrong part of the sentence.

ORIGINAL

Shelly took the infant, who had just had a baby, to San Francisco. (The infant had a baby? Not likely—even in California.)

REVISION

Shelly, who had just had a baby, took the infant to San Francisco. (The modifier is now properly placed.)

ORIGINAL

The man chased the chicken with
a butcher knife, which was so
scared it ran right at him. (The
butcher knife was scared?)

REVISION

With a butcher knife, the man
chased the chicken, which was so
scared it ran right at him.

Note how the writer changes the meaning of each sentence
below by shifting the modifier *only*:

I *only* asked her for a dollar.

Only I asked her for a dollar.

I asked her *only* for a dollar.

I asked her for a dollar *only*.

Numbers—Use Arabic numerals for numbers in dates; addresses; telephone numbers; hours and minutes written as A.M. or P.M.; decimals; certain travel information; certain data about books; and all other numbers that cannot be written in one or two words. For most other uses, spell out the number instead of writing it in Arabic numerals.

1. Dates:

   January 1, 1981

   October 14, 1942

   July 4
   (*Not* July 4th but July Fourth; likewise, January first and October fourteenth)

2. Addresses:

   5747 Giddings Street, Chicago, Illinois 60091

   Room 2335, 1600 Market Street
   San Francisco, California 94102

Apt. 34, the Grandeur Hotel
600 Granville Avenue
New York, New York 10022

3. Telephone numbers:

415-346-8105

592-6871

4. Hours and minutes used with A.M. or P.M.:

4:00 P.M.

8:00 A.M.
(*Not* 8 o'clock; rather eight o'clock)

5. Decimals:

98.6°

3.1416

6. Certain travel information:

Highway 80 is one of our finest freeways.

TWA flight 134 boards at gate 51.

7. Certain data about books:

The information can be found in paragraph 12 (lines 8–10) on p. 260 of *Rhetoric in a Modern Mode*.

8.   All other numbers that cannot be written as one or two words:

ORIGINAL

She was *19* on February 24, 1981.

There were exactly *fifty-nine thousand six hundred and eighty-seven* fans at her last rock concert.

REVISION

She was *nineteen* on February 24, 1981.

There were exactly *59,687* fans at her last rock concert.

Exception

Never begin sentences with numerals.

ORIGINAL

800 students enthusiastically applauded his last lecture.

REVISION

Eight hundred students enthusiastically applauded his last lecture.

If necessary, rewrite the sentence in order to avoid beginning it with a numeral:

ORIGINAL

2615 Park Boulevard was his address in those years.

REVISION

His address in those years was 2615 Park Boulevard.

Organization—Organize each formal essay so that there is a systematic order of events, details, and ideas.

Since the paragraph can be treated as an essay in miniature, you can greatly improve the organization of your essays by studying the following approach to the organization of the paragraph. In addition, you will find that many of your problems with organization lie in poorly organized paragraphs within the body of the essay itself.

Natural order

For some subjects use natural order. There are two kinds of natural order: *the order of space* and *the order of time.*

1. The Order of Space

Whenever an assignment requires that you describe a concrete object—a face, a room, the cover of a magazine, a landscape—your subject contains a natural arrangement: *the order of space.* A room, for instance, can be described in a clockwise or a counterclockwise direction; from the inside or the outside; from the center or a corner; from a fixed or a moving point; from the floor to the ceiling. A person can be described from head to foot; from foot to head; from a central point to either extremity. In other words, *the order of space shows how elements are related to each other in space; such order is built into assignments requiring that you describe things or people.*

Look at a simple example first. The next paragraph uses the order of space to arrange details in the description of a landscape. Notice that the narrator is the focal point:

The December grass on the island was blanched and sere, pale against the dusty boles of sycamores, noisy under foot. *Behind me,* the way I had come, rose the pasture belonging to Twilight, a horse of perpetually different color whose name was originally Midnight, and who one spring startled the neighborhood by becoming brown. Far *before me* Tinker Mountain glinted and pitched in the sunlight. The Lucas orchard spanned the *middle distance,* its wan peach limbs swept and poised just so, row upon row, like a stageful of thin innocent dancers who will never be asked to perform; *below* the orchard rolled the steers' pasture yielding to flood plain fields and finally the sycamore log bridge to the island where in horror I had watched a green frog sucked to a skin and sunk. A fugitive,

empty sky vaulted *overhead*, apparently receding
from me the harder I searched its dome for a measure
of distance.

> —Annie Dillard, *Pilgrim at Tinker Creek*
> (New York: Harper's Magazine Press, 1974)

Then look at a more complex example: A. E. Hotchner's
description of Ernest Hemingway. Hotchner scans
Hemingway's appearance in this order: pants, belt, shirt,
shoes, hair, and mustache. Next, in some detail, he
describes the dominant impression: Hemingway was
"massive." Finally, Hotchner concludes with a much
more important point: Hemingway "radiated" *enjoyment*.
Despite the complexity of this paragraph, the arrangement
of details is both interesting and clear:

Hemingway . . . was wearing khaki pants held up by a
wide old leather belt with a huge buckle inscribed
GOTT MIT UNS, a white linen sport shirt that hung
loose, and brown leather loafers without socks. His
hair was dark with gray highlights, flecked white at
the temples, and he had a heavy mustache that ran
past the corners of his mouth, but no beard. He was
massive. Not in height, for he was only an inch over
six feet, but in impact. Most of his two hundred
pounds was concentrated above his waist: he had
square heavy shoulders, long hugely muscled arms
(the left one jaggedly scarred and a bit misshapen at

the elbow), a deep chest, a belly-rise but no hips or
thighs. Something played off him—he was intense,
electrokinetic, but in control, a race horse reined in.
He stopped to talk to one of the musicians in fluent
Spanish and something about him hit me—
enjoyment: God, I thought, how he's *enjoying*
himself! I had never seen anyone with such an aura of
fun and well-being. He radiated it and everyone in the
place responded. He had so much more in his face
than I had expected to find from seeing his
photographs.

—A. E. Hotchner, *Papa Hemingway*
(New York: Random House, 1966, p. 6)

2.   The Order of Time

Less frequently you will meet subjects with another kind
of natural order—*the order of time.*

When you are asked to write a narrative, a story, or an
anecdote, you will need to use the order of time—to show
how things happened one after another *in time.* To do
that, simply describe what happened, selecting details for
interest, of course, and using words like *first, next, then,*
and *finally* to show the chronological relationship of
events.

Here is a beautiful example: George Orwell's story of
shooting an elephant. The elephant, temporarily mad, had

killed a native; and as a member of the Indian Imperial Police, Orwell had the job of finding the beast and killing him. He writes:

> When I pulled the trigger I did not hear the bang or feel the kick—one never does when a shot goes home—but I heard the devilish roar of glee that went up from the crowd. In that instant, in too short a time, one would have thought, even for the bullet to get there, a mysterious, terrible change had come over the elephant. He neither stirred nor fell, but every line of his body had altered. He looked suddenly stricken, shrunken, immensely old, as though the frightful impact of the bullet had paralyzed him without knocking him down. At last, after what seemed a long time—it might have been five seconds, I dare say—he sagged flabbily to his knees. His mouth slobbered. An enormous senility seemed to have settled upon him. One could have imagined him thousands of years old. I fired again into the same spot. At the second shot he did not collapse but climbed with desperate slowness to his feet and stood weakly upright, with legs sagging and head dropping. I fired a third time. That was the shot that did it for him. You could see the agony of it jolt his whole body and knock the last remnant of strength from his legs. But in falling he seemed for a moment to rise, for as his hind legs collapsed beneath him he seemed to tower upwards like a huge rock toppling, his trunk reaching skywards like a tree. He

trumpeted for his first and only time. And then down
he came, his belly towards me, with a crash that
seemed to shake the ground even where I lay.

> —George Orwell, "Shooting an Elephant,"
> *Shooting an Elephant and Other Essays*
> (New York: Harcourt Brace Jovanovich, 1945)

Remember, then: *to organize a narrative, use the
natural order—the order of time.*

Logical order

Besides the natural orders of space and time, there is only
one other kind of clear organization: *logical order.*

Logical order simplifies complex ideas and gives shape
to formless impressions; it reduces a chaotic swirl of
thoughts to a smooth and intelligible flow of connected
ideas. It is the essential ingredient of good expository
prose.

For most subjects, you can use one of three
kinds of logical order: *analysis, classification,
comparison-contrast.*

1.   Analysis

Analysis is the process of dividing a whole into its parts; it
is a way of "loosening up" anything to separate it into its
basic elements or internal divisions.

The following paragraph, for example, analyzes the three parts of an atom.

> The atom has long been defined as the smallest part of an element that has all the characteristics of that element. This definition is still true but in the present century scientists have discovered that the atom itself consists of three kinds of still smaller particles. The particles spinning in orbit around the nucleus are called *electrons*. Each electron carries a charge of negative electricity, exactly the same amount for all electrons. In the nucleus of the atom are *protons* and *neutrons*. Each proton carries a charge of positive electricity exactly equal to the negative charge of an electron. The proton, however, is 1,845 times as heavy as the electron. The neutron, as its name implies, carries no electricity, but it weighs slightly more than the proton.

> —Adapted from Samuel Namowitz and Donald Stone,
> *Earth Science: The World We Live In,* 4th ed.
> (New York: American Book Co., 1969, p. 12)

2. Classification

Another common and useful kind of logical order is *classification. Classification works by sorting things into groups.* It is so closely related to analysis that it is sometimes seen as an aspect of the same process, but there is a difference. While analysis divides a whole into its parts, classification brings together similar things to show what they have in common. You will understand the difference if you first analyze and then classify something—a magazine, for instance. If you *analyze* a magazine, you take it apart in some systematic way; if you *classify* a magazine, you place it in a category with other magazines. For example, if you *analyze Time*, you can find that it is divided into sixteen to twenty-two sections (Nation, People, Television, Sport, etc.). But if you *classify Time*, you can group it with other weekly news magazines—*Newsweek* and *U. S. News & World Report*, for example.

Note how analysis and classification work together in the following paragraphs. In the first, psychologist Eric Berne divides the tube formed by a human embryo into three layers and discusses the development of each layer. In the second paragraph, he classifies human beings according to three corresponding types.

> Everyone knows that a human being, like a chicken, comes from an egg. At a very early stage, the human embryo forms a three-layered tube, the inside layer of which grows into the stomach and lungs, the middle layer into bones, muscles, joints, and blood vessels, and the outside layer into the skin and nervous system. . . .
> We can thus say that while the average human being is a mixture, some people are mainly "digestion-minded," some "muscle-minded," and

some "brain-minded," and correspondingly digestion-bodied, muscle-bodied, or brain-bodied. The digestion-bodied people look thick; the muscle-bodied people look wide; and the brain-bodied people look long. This does not mean the taller a man is the brainier he will be. It means that if a man, even a short man, looks long rather than wide or thick, he will often be more concerned about what goes on in his mind than about what he does or what he eats; but the key factor is slenderness and not height. On the other hand, a man who gives the impression of being thick rather than long or wide will usually be more interested in a good steak than in a good idea or a good long walk.

—Eric Berne, *A Layman's Guide to Psychology and Psychoanalysis* (New York: Simon & Schuster, 1947)

3. Comparison-Contrast

A third kind of logical order is *comparison-contrast. Comparison points out similarities; contrast points out differences.* Often, however, we use both comparison and contrast to organize a discussion of things that are different in some ways and similar in others. For the sake of convenience—and because they have much in common—let's speak of the three processes as *comparison-contrast.*

Use *comparison* to analyze two (or more) things at one time in order to show their *similarities*.

Use *contrast* to analyze two (or more) things at the same time in order to show their *differences*.

Use *comparison-contrast* to analyze two (or more) things that are *different* in some ways and *similar* in other ways.

The Paragraph of Comparison. Study the following paragraph as an example. It comes from an essay entitled "James Bond: Culture Hero," by George Grella. Grella's thesis is that Bond's popularity rests not on his competence as a hero (actually, Bond is incredibly *incompetent*) but on the resemblance of the Bond novels to "historic epic and romance, based on the stuff of myth and legend." In the following paragraph Grella compares the situation in the novel *Moonraker* with the myth of "Perseus-St. George."*

In *Moonraker* [by Ian Fleming] the situation parallels the Perseus-St. George myth, an appropriate one for Bond's rescue of London from the great rocket of Sir Hugo Drax, the huge dragon menacing England. Drax has red hair, an ugly, burned face which even plastic

---

* Perseus, in Greek mythology, was the son of Zeus and Danaë and slayer of the wicked Medusa. He married Andromeda after rescuing her from a sea monster (dragon). St. George, patron saint of England, saved a king's daughter from a dragon (according to legend). This story, it is widely believed, may have been "borrowed" from the story of Perseus' battle with the monster that threatened Andromeda. In myth and legend the two stories are often connected.

surgery cannot mask, splayed "ogre's teeth"; the great
burst of fire he hopes to turn on London is the modern
equivalent of the dragon's flames. Fleming employs an
ironic reversal of one aspect of the Perseus myth;
instead of rescuing Andromeda from the cliff where
she is chained; Bond and his Andromeda, Galatea
Brand, are nearly killed when one of the Dover cliffs,
with some urging from Drax, falls on them. Of course
Bond survives and, after escaping steamhosing and
the liftoff of the Moonraker rocket (more fire from the
dragon's nostrils), saves London. Alone among Bond
novels, the hero fails to get the girl at the end: as a
modern St. George, it would scarcely be appropriate
for him to win the fair maiden.

—George Grella, "James Bond: Culture Hero"
(*The New Republic*, May 30, 1964)

The Paragraph of Contrast. Use contrast to analyze two
(or more) things at the same time in order to show their
differences, as in the following paragraph contrasting
European and American cities. The main idea, stated in
the first sentence, lists three important differences. Each
of these differences is taken up in turn in the body of the
paragraph:

European cities—French cities in particular—are
crowded in ways American cities are not: most
buildings are multi-story; no room is left between
buildings; and buildings are flush with the sidewalk.

First, most buildings are multi-story. In cities such as Paris, Chartres, even places as small as Avalon, it is hard to tell a residence from an office building. Buildings are three, four, five stories at least, especially if they contain apartments—which the French often buy as homes. There seem to be no one-story dwellings such as we so commonly see in residential areas in the U.S. Secondly, each building is flung right up against the next: there is not even room for a passageway. In Paris one can walk for blocks without seeing daylight except in the "canyons"—the streets themselves. It doesn't matter whether it's a residential or business area. In America, however, most residential and business areas offer at least a little open space. Finally, there are no lawns and very few trees in front of European buildings: they are flush with the sidewalk. Most houses in America, of course, are set back from the street and the sidewalk, leaving room for grass, trees, or some other form of greenery. While it is true that fine architecture may be enough to compensate for lack of space and greenery, it is interesting to note that given any excuse, the typical Parisian flees to the country: as one of them put it, "The trees, the greenery, the space—ah, you Americans are so very fortunate."

The Paragraph of Comparison and Contrast. Use comparison and contrast to analyze two (or more) things that are different in some ways, and similar in other ways.

Here is an excellent example—a paragraph that compares *and* contrasts our now-departed "hippies" with the subculture that came before them, the "beats." The main idea, again, is stated in the first sentence: "there has been a startling transformation in bohemia." The first sentence leads into a brief discussion of *similarities* between hippies and beats; these similarities are developed in a few details. The third sentence introduces a discussion of the *differences*; these are developed in several details. Again, there is no summary sentence, but the pattern closely resembles that of the model paragraph of analysis.

The immediate progenitors of the hippies were the beats of the 1950s, but there has been a startling transformation in bohemia. Many of the same elements were present in the beat generation: scorn for prevailing sexual mores, a predilection for pot and peyote, wanderlust, a penchant for Oriental mysticism on the order of Zen and the Veda. Yet the contrasts are even more striking. San Francisco's North Beach was a study in black and white; the Haight-Ashbury is a crazy quilt of living color. Black was a basic color in the abstract-expressionist painting of the beats; hippiedom's psychedelic poster art is blindingly vivid. The progressive jazz of the beats was coolly cerebral; the acid rock of the hippies is as visceral as a torn intestine.

—"The Hippies" (*Time*, July 7, 1967, p. 20)

Arranging Details in Comparison-Contrast Paragraphs. In paragraphs organized by comparison-contrast, place your details in one of two ways: *"point-by-point"* or *"block-by-block."*

Suppose for example that you are contrasting European and American cities. You can discuss the differences between them point-by-point, or you can discuss European cities in one part of your paragraph and American cities in the next. You might make a rough outline showing the arrangement of details in each of these two plans:

POINT-BY-POINT ORGANIZATION

| European cities | multistory buildings |
| American cities | many single-story buildings |

| European cities | usually no room between buildings |
| American cities | usually some room between buildings |

| European cities | buildings flush with sidewalk |
| American cities | buildings set back from sidewalk |

BLOCK-BY-BLOCK ORGANIZATION

| European cities | multistory buildings
usually no room between buildings
buildings flush with sidewalk |
| American cities | many single-story buildings
usually some room between buildings
buildings set back from sidewalk |

In writing the paragraph organized point-by-point, you would discuss one point at a time, dealing with European cities in one sentence (or more) and with American cities in the next sentence(s). Look back at the model paragraph to see how that is done.

The paragraph organized point-by-point is usually clearer and sharper, but the paragraph organized block-by-block is by no means uncommon. Suppose for example that you are contrasting the culture of the Pueblo Indians with that of the Dobus (who live on the Dobu Island off the coast of New Guinea). In writing a paragraph organized block-by-block, you would discuss the Pueblos in the first part of the paragraph and the Dobus in the next part, like this:

> According to Ruth Benedict in *Patterns of Culture*, the Pueblo Indians are different from the Dobus in three important ways. Take the Pueblos first. The Pueblos have a very cooperative, peaceful society. They are not jealous about sexual rights and they do not punish infidelity. Moreover, they make no display of political or economic power. The Dobus are different in every way. To begin with, they are violent, aggressive people. Unlike the Pueblos, they are intensely jealous: the in-laws spy on married people constantly, and any infidelity is met with swift, brutal punishment. Also, the Dobus are fiercely proud of political and economic success: like the old-time

Captains of American Industry, they worship property
and will go to any extreme—including fraud and
murder—to get what they want.

By now you should see for yourself which of the two
arrangements works best: differences (or similarities) are
sharper and clearer when the details are arranged
point-by-point. *For most comparison-contrast
paragraphs, then, use a point-by-point arrangement.*

Outline—Make an outline to organize the structure and
content of your paper or to see that your paper follows an
order that will be clear to your reader.

o|

Despite any former resistance you may have had to
making outlines, remember that they can save you time in
the long run and help you get a better grade. Suppose, for
example, you are assigned a paper and have settled on a
thesis. What do you do next? After gathering information,
you probably jot down the main ideas or topics you will
use to support your thesis. You have, in fact, begun to
make a rough outline. Now you can quickly see what facts,
examples, etc. will fit under each main idea; you will also
see which ones do *not* fit your paper and should be
discarded.

If your composition is short or informal and an outline has not been assigned, you may decide to skip the outline. However, once you have completed the first draft it is a good idea to outline it to see if it is well organized and easy to follow—or if you have jumbled your points or left out something important.

Make a formal outline first when you are writing a long formal paper or when an outline is required by your instructor. There are two kinds of formal outlines: the *topic outline* and the *sentence outline*. In making a topic outline, you will use only a word or phrase for each of your divisions; for example, "A. Three causes of inflation." In formulating a sentence outline, you will use a complete sentence for each division; for example, "A. There are three causes of inflation." (Very often the main ideas or topics of a sentence outline will become the topic sentences of the paragraphs in your final paper.)

Here is the format for a formal outline—either topic or sentence—of a typical paper. Use Roman numerals (I, II, III . . .) for main topics, capital letters (A, B, C . . .) for subtopics, Arabic numerals (1, 2, 3 . . .) for sub-subtopics, and small letters (a, b, c . . .) for supporting material for any sub-subtopics. Indent your divisions like this:

THESIS

  I. Introduction

 II. First Main Idea or Topic (support of thesis)

    A.   Subtopic (support of main idea)

    B.   Subtopic

    C.   Subtopic

III. Second Main Idea or Topic

    A.   Subtopic

        1.   Sub-subtopic (support of subtopic)

        2.   Sub-subtopic

    B.   Subtopic

IV. Third Main Idea or Topic

    A.   Subtopic

    B.   Subtopic

        1.   Sub-subtopic

            a.   Support of Sub-subtopic

            b.   Support of Sub-subtopic

        2.   Sub-subtopic

V. Conclusion

Note: Just as no entity can be divided into one part, unless a division of your outline can be broken into *two* or *more* parts, you cannot further divide it; that is, you cannot have an *A* without a *B*, a *1* without a *2*, and so on.

Following is a topic outline for a student paper about an American institution.

THESIS: America has a love affair with the hamburger.

I.   Introduction

II. Origin and route to the United States

    A.   Raw meat scraped and shredded by Tartars on Russian steppes

    B.   Technique carried to Hamburg by German sailors

    C.   Practice brought to United States by German immigrants

III. America's best-sellers

    A.   MacDonald's

        1.   Assembly-line production

        2.   Merchandising methods

    B.   Burger King, Burger Chef, and other franchises

IV. Advantages of making one's own hamburgers

    A.   Saves money

    B.   Insures quality

        1.   How to choose best meat

          a.   Red, slightly flecked with white
          b.   20% to 25% fat
    2.   How to grind for best flavor

V. Conclusion

Parallel Structure—Use parallel grammatical
constructions for ideas of equal importance and similar
function.

Parallel means "closely agreeing in essential qualities and
characteristics." Grammatical constructions are parallel
when they have a likeness or similarity that permits them
to be labeled with the same grammatical tag: "noun
clauses"; "prepositional phrases"; "present participles."
    Parallel ideas are often joined by "correlative"
conjunctions or other "correlative" words, such as *both
. . . and, not only . . . but also, not . . . but, either . . . or,
neither . . . nor, some . . . others,* and *the one . . . the other.*
Such words are called "correlative" because they
"co-relate": they convey natural, reciprocal relationships
between the ideas and between the constructions that
contain the ideas.
    Some writing assignments, you should note, require a
one-sentence statement of the main idea, *phrased so as to
list or enumerate each point to be discussed.* This

sentence must be preeminently clear and correct. In particular, the elements listed in the sentence should be stated *in parallel grammatical form:* you should use three words, or three phrases, or three clauses.

The following sentence, for example, is badly phrased because the elements are not expressed in parallel grammatical form: "There are three things I like about my job: *the hours, the pay,* and *it is interesting work.*" Correctly phrased, the sentence reads: "There are three things I like about my job: *the hours fit my schedule, the pay is good,* and *the work is very interesting.*"

The sentences below illustrate some of the writer's options for the one-sentence statement of the main idea:

Parallel words

San Francisco is a city with something for everyone: culture, recreation, and atmosphere.

Parallel phrases

You *can* live on next to nothing by growing most of your own food, by dressing simply, and by reducing all other material needs to a true minimum.

Parallel clauses

There are three advantages of being a bachelor: you are free to do as you wish; you can date as many different women as you like; and you need not worry about a family.

The problems—and strengths—of parallel constructions require careful study. In the examples below, note in particular the grace and force parallel structures may bring to your writing.

1. Maintain parallel structure in a series of words, phrases, or clauses:

Words

ORIGINAL

Dieting, running, and *the gym* barely keep me in shape. (In this series, *the gym* is not parallel with the two gerunds *dieting* and *running*.)

REVISION

Dieting, running, and *exercising at the gym* barely keep me in shape. (The three gerunds are parallel.)

Phrases

ORIGINAL

We walked everywhere in Paris that summer—*through the parks, across the bridges of the Seine, down the broad boulevards,* and

REVISION

We walked everywhere in Paris that summer—*through the parks, across the bridges of the Seine, down the broad boulevards,* and *ate at sidewalk cafes.* (*Ate at sidewalk cafes*, a verbal phrase, is not parallel in grammar or in thought to the prepositional phrases to which it is attached.)

past sidewalk cafes, where we often stopped to eat escargots and to watch the other walkers. (*Past sidewalk cafes*, a prepositional phrase, is now parallel in thought and grammar to the other prepositional phrases in this sentence. The adjective clause that follows is grammatically correct; it simply adds another idea to the sentence.)

Clauses

ORIGINAL

The sun rose early, we crawled out of our tents, and *on some days all the way to the creek.* (*On some days all the way to the creek* is not a clause; in grammar and in thought it is not parallel to the other two elements in this sentence.)

REVISION

The sun rose early, we crawled out of our tents, and then *we dashed down to the creek*, though on some days we felt like crawling. (*We dashed down to the creek*, a main clause, is now parallel in grammar and thought to the other main clauses in this sentence. The adverb clause that follows is grammatically correct; it simply adds another idea to the sentence.)

2.   Occasionally use parallel structure for rhetorical effect:

As a poetic device, parallel structure can be used occasionally with great force in English prose. Consider, for example, the following passage from Dr. Johnson's famous letter to the Earl of Chesterfield, written in February of 1755, just after Dr. Johnson had published his great *Dictionary*. Chesterfield, who had been cold and distant when Johnson had first approached him, was now offering to be Johnson's "patron." Johnson rejected the offer in the following terms, using parallel phrases most effectively: "Is not a Patron, my Lord, one who looks with unconcern on a man struggling for life in the water, and, when he has reached ground, encumbers him with help? The notice which you have been pleased to take of my labours, had it been early, had been kind; but it has been delayed *till I am indifferent, and cannot enjoy it; till I am solitary, and cannot impart it; till I am known, and do not want it.*"

3.   Occasionally use parallel structure to achieve unity and coherence:

As a device of repetition, parallel structure can be used to achieve unity and coherence. In his "Inaugural Address," delivered January 20, 1961, President John F. Kennedy approached a vast subject—his hope for the future of mankind—and handled it with deceptive ease by setting up a number of parallel series. He begins one group of paragraphs in the following ways:

"To those old allies. . . ."

"To those new states. . . ."

"To those peoples. . . ."

"To our sister republics. . . ."

"To that world assembly of sovereign states. . . ."

"Finally, to those nations. . . ."

He begins another group of paragraphs thus:

"So let us begin anew. . . ."

"Let both sides explore. . . ."

"Let both sides, for the first time, formulate. . . ."

"Let both sides seek. . . ."

"Let both sides unite. . . ."

"And if a beachhead of cooperation may push back the jungle of suspicion, let both sides join. . . ."

The parallel structure and the repetition give the "Inaugural Address" unity and coherence—and force—that the President could have achieved in no other way.

Caution: A common error in parallel structure involves comparisons. For example:

"I am *taller* than *anyone* in this room."

Logically, that statement is absurd, since the speaker, who is presumably in the room himself, cannot be taller than *anyone* in the room: he can only be taller than *anyone else* in the room.

In comparisons, then, *exclude the things compared from other members of the group:*

ORIGINAL

Jackie is a better putter than *any* golfer I know. (This statement is illogical, unless the speaker does not know Jackie at all.)

REVISION

Jackie is a better putter than *any other* golfer I know.

---

paren   **Parentheses**—Use parentheses only when you want to separate certain parenthetical elements (those related but not essential to the meaning of a sentence) from the rest of the sentence.

One of three devices can be used to set off parenthetical elements: commas, which provide normal separation; dashes, which provide the most emphatic separation; and

parentheses, which provide less emphatic separation.
Parentheses also have certain special functions.

1.   Use parentheses for clearly emphatic clauses and
phrases that you feel require distinct separation from the
rest of the sentence:

> She admired the dress (though at the moment a mere
> thirty hung in her closet) and asked if she might try it
> on.

2.   Use parentheses to set off dates, references, and
figures in an enumeration:

> *Dates*
>
> Harriet Martineau (1802–1876), an English visitor,
> wrote complimentary things about American manners
> as she found them in 1832.

> *References*
>
> Organizing a paragraph is no difficult thing if you
> know what you are doing (see *Rhetoric in a Modern
> Mode*, Ch. 3).

> *Figures in an Enumeration*
>
> She charged her husband with three responsibilities:
> (1) keeping house; (2) keeping the children out of
> trouble; (3) keeping up with her intellectually.

Caution: Punctuate in and around parentheses correctly.
(a)   Use appropriate end punctuation within the parentheses if the first word begins with a capital letter:

P. T. Barnum was the king of humbug and the creator of hoaxes. (But he wrote that it is debt that robs a young man of self-respect.)

(b)   Use semicolons, colons, and commas when they are necessary after the second parenthesis. Do not use them before it or before an opening parenthesis except in enumeration:

ORIGINAL	REVISION
There was algae growing in the bottle (which had been filled at Walden Pond;) as a result, the bottle made a strange-looking paperweight.	There was algae growing in the bottle (which had been filled at Walden Pond); as a result, the bottle made a strange-looking paperweight.
Richard Henry Dana, Jr., had well-developed antislavery feelings (he legally sought to prevent the return of at least two runaway slaves:) he was determined to thwart the Fugitive Slave Law.	Richard Henry Dana, Jr., had well-developed antislavery feelings (he legally sought to prevent the return of at least two runaway slaves): he was determined to thwart the Fugitive Slave Law.

Note: For the use of question marks in parentheses to cast doubt, see **Question Mark.** For related but distinctly different marks of punctuation, see **Brackets** and **Dash.** Note in particular that brackets most often enclose editorial comment; that dashes emphasize parenthetical material; and that parentheses de-emphasize such material.

Passive Constructions—Avoid passive constructions whenever possible.

pass

Passive constructions are subject-verb combinations in which the subject is acted upon by an agent that may or may not be identified after the verb:

Like impersonal constructions, passive constructions are not *bad*—they are weak: instead of *acting*, the subject *is acted upon*. Passive constructions are also wordy, simply because they demand more words than active constructions. Finally, since passive constructions may omit the agent, they are vague: often we do not learn who performed the action.

A significant point? It is especially significant in expository and argumentative writing: passive constructions permit—or sometimes encourage—the writer to shun his responsibility to be specific and authoritative. "It is well known that . . ." may sound persuasive, even though the assertion has no substance to it. "The fact has been widely acknowledged that . . ." may not state a fact at all.

In other words, passive constructions are weak, vague, evasive, and often underhanded—if not actively dishonest. Do not use them unless you must.

PASSIVE	ACTIVE
The workers were warned by the managers to be on time.	*The managers warned* the workers to be on time.
It has been announced that *classes will be dismissed* for the rally.	The *president has announced* that *he will dismiss* classes for the rally.

(See **Impersonal Construction** and **Sentence Structure/ Style.**)

---

p

Period—Use a period at the end of most sentences and non-sentences, for decimals, after abbreviations, and for ellipsis dots.

1.   Use a period at the end of declarative and imperative sentences and sentences that ask indirect questions:

Declarative Sentence

The shortest route to San Francisco is Route 5.

Imperative Sentence

Drive forward to the first pump for quicker service.

Indirect Question

She asked if he could drive her to New York.

2. Use a period after non-sentence salutations and answers to questions:

Good morning.

Hello.

Where are we going? To the supermarket to get steaks for our barbecue.

3. Use a period for decimals:

The ratio of the circumference of a circle to its diameter, known as pi (π), is a transcendental number having a value, to eight decimal places, of 3.14159265.

On this campus you can obtain only 3.2 beer.

4. Use a period after abbreviations:

Mr. Snippet

Ms. Moppet

N.Y.

Do not, however, use a period after the abbreviations (initials) of many agencies, institutions, and organized groups (FBI, CIA, UNESCO, NAACP).

(See **Abbreviations.**)

5. Use periods for ellipsis marks.

(See **Ellipsis.**)

Note: Always place the period *inside* quotation marks, whether the period belongs to the quoted part or to the sentence as a whole:

I have just finished reading Chekhov's great story "The Kiss."

(See **Quotation Marks.**)

---

plag

Plagiarism—Do not use the words or ideas of another to create in your reader's mind the false belief that the words and ideas are your own.

Anyone who writes needs a working definition of *plagiarism.* Experienced writers usually understand what constitutes plagiarism in a given context. They understand the fine differences between plagiarism, borrowing, and imitation, and they have the training and experience that allows them to use the work of other writers fairly and properly. They know how to paraphrase, how to quote, and how to document their sources with clear references in the text, with footnotes, and with bibliographical information.

Student writers, however, often lack the training they need to guide them in these matters. Some students are confused about the difference between legitimate research and plagiarism. In rare instances, it is possible for a student to appear to be plagiarizing when he or she is merely ignorant of proper writing practices, especially since earlier instruction in writing may have encouraged copying or paraphrasing without regard to such technical matters as quotation marks and footnotes.

What Is Plagiarism?

To plagiarize is "to steal and use (the ideas or writings of another) as one's own" or "to appropriate passages or ideas (from another) and use them as one's own" (*American Heritage Dictionary*).

Plagiarism is literary theft. A writer commits plagiarism by deliberately—or even unwittingly—creating in the reader's mind the false belief that the words and ideas are the writer's own when, in fact, they are not.

Plagiarism is a serious academic offense, viewed, at its best, as cheating—and, at its worse, as a crime more offensive than shoplifting or burglary. Such cheating affects the student's own academic development and is always unfair to other students and to the instructor.

Consequently, plagiarism may result in severe discipline, depending on the circumstances and on the policies of your school.

Some Examples of Plagiarism

The following acts must be viewed as plagiarism:

1.   The writer steals not only facts and ideas but phrases, whole sentences, and longer passages from published work and presents them as his or her own. The writer does not use quotation marks to set off the parts that are quoted word for word or repeated with only minor variations in phrasing.

The writer also omits *documentation*—important details about the source, such as the author's name, the title of the publication, and the relevant page numbers.

The omission of such details creates the false belief in the reader's mind that the words used are the writer's own when, in fact, they are not.

2.   The writer steals an entire work or an entire passage from a longer work and presents it as his or her own. In

one case, a student memorized six full paragraphs from a reference book and wrote them word for word from memory on an examination that was being used to test the student's writing ability. Even though the student did not "copy" from an open book or from notes during the examination, his work was clearly plagiarism since the quoted material tended to create in the reader's mind the false belief that the ideas and words were the writer's own when, in fact, they were not.

3.   A student buys a paper written by a professional ghostwriter.

4.   A student hands in a paper written by a former student.

5.   A student hands in a paper written, in whole or in part, by a friend or a relative.

In each of these instances the writer creates the false belief that the words used are the writer's own when in fact they are not. Each case constitutes plagiarism. And each may be detected and punished.

How to Avoid Plagiarism

Plagiarism that results from ignorance of correct writing techniques can be avoided by careful documentation.

Writers should learn to incorporate information about their sources into their actual writing and to add details in footnotes and a bibliography.

For a complete explanation of these techniques, see the section on The Research Paper, pages 225–61.

Question Mark—Use the question mark when you ask a direct question or in parentheses when you want to express doubt or uncertainty.

Direct Question

Where were you on the night of August 14, 1980?

You promised to have this paper in on time, didn't you?

Doubt or Uncertainty

The brilliant (?) speaker alternately annoyed and bored his audience.

Wallace Stevens' poem "The Emperor of Ice-Cream," written in 1923 (?), uses symbolic figures to suggest the vulgar inevitability of death.

Note: If a direct question occurs as part of a quotation, or in the form of a quotation, place the question mark *within* the quotation mark.

ORIGINAL

"Is the plane on schedule," she
asked?

REVISION

"Is the plane on schedule?" she
asked.

If the entire sentence is a question, however, place the
question mark at the end of the sentence, *after* the
quotation mark.

ORIGINAL

Did you hear him say, "I'll be
home by two o'clock?"

Have you read Chekhov's story
"The Kiss?"

REVISION

Did you hear him say, "I'll be
home by two o'clock"?

Have you read Chekhov's story
"The Kiss"?

Caution: Do not use a question mark with an *indirect*
question.

ORIGINAL

She asked where the jelly beans
were? (This is correct only if you
are asking—with some
disbelief—whether she asked.)

REVISION

She asked where the jelly beans
were.

---

quot   **Quotation Marks**—Use quotation marks around all direct
quotations from printed material; all quoted dialogue; and

the titles of short stories, brief poems, songs, essays, reviews, book chapters, and unpublished manuscripts.

In general, there are two types of quotations: *direct* and *indirect*. The direct quotation sets off the exact words of the speaker or the writer in quotation marks. The indirect quotation, however, is a paraphrase of those words, often introduced by the word *that* (which may be either expressed or implied), and takes no quotation marks.

DIRECT	INDIRECT
I asked, "How long has she been dead, Bruno?"	I asked Bruno how long she had been dead.
"I don't know," he said.	He said (that) he didn't know.

1.   Use quotation marks around all direct quotations from printed material:

> In *ABC of Reading*, published in 1934, Ezra Pound wrote: "To go back to the beginning of history, you probably know that there is spoken language and written language, and that there are two kinds of written language, one based on sound, the other on sight."

Note: Long, formal quotations are introduced by colons; shorter, less formal quotations are introduced by commas.

(see **Colon, Comma,** and **Dialogue.**)

2.   Use quotation marks to set off quoted dialogue:

I got close enough to him to smell the garlic and red wine and to see that, as usual, though he looked as though he had not shaved in two days, he had cut himself very recently with a razor. I got really close—close enough to see the open pores in the big nose, and the little red eyes, and the big ears up tight against the greasy dark hair.

I said, "You're crazy, Bruno!"

"Lieutenant, you bore me," he said. "Go scare some kiddies."

(a)   Be careful not to omit the second set of quotation marks:

"I'm leaving right now," she said.

"I do not object to your language," I said, "but I do object to your ideas."

(b)   Always place the verb of saying *outside* the quotation marks:

She said, "I'll do exactly as I please."

"I'll do exactly as I please," she said.

"I'll do," she said, "exactly as I please."

(c)   Use commas to set off the verb of saying:

I said, "Shut up!"

(Compare the indirect quotation: *I said that he should shut up.*)

"The same to you," he replied.

"I can't do it," I said, "but you can."

(d)   When the verb of saying comes after the quoted dialogue, do not use a comma if the quotation itself ends in a question mark or an exclamation point:

"Shut up!" he said.

"Oh, won't you?" I asked.

(Note that the sentence itself ends with a period.)

(e)   The verb of saying is sometimes omitted:

"Do you love me?"

"Of course, darling! What do you take me for?"

"I don't know. . . . Sometimes I'm so unsure."

(f)   Written dialogue represents the directly quoted speech of usually two or more persons talking together. It is standard practice, however, to write each person's speech, no matter how short, as a separate paragraph. Related bits of narration, including verbs of saying, are customarily presented in the paragraph along with the speech.

There was a long pause.

"Is that all?" Alice timidly asked.

"That's all," said Humpty Dumpty. "Good-bye."

This was rather sudden, Alice thought: but, after such a very strong hint that she ought to be going, she felt that it would hardly be civil to stay. So she got up, and held out her hand. "Good-bye, till we meet again!" she said as cheerfully as she could.

"I shouldn't know you again if we *did* meet," Humpty Dumpty replied in a discontented tone, giving her one of his fingers to shake: "you're so exactly like other people."

—Lewis Carroll, *Through the Looking-Glass*

(See **Dialogue** for a discussion of dialogue per se.)

3.   Use quotation marks around the titles of short stories, brief poems, songs, essays, reviews, book chapters, and unpublished manuscripts:

Short Stories

"The Diamond as Big as the Ritz" is one of F. Scott Fitzgerald's best short stories.

Brief Poems

Along with many other young romantics, she memorized John Keats' "Ode on a Grecian Urn."

(BUT: Milton's *Paradise Lost* is certainly a long poem.)

Songs

"White Christmas" is maudlin but still rather nice.

Essays (reviews, book chapters, and other brief prose compositions)

Jonathan Swift's "A Modest Proposal for Preventing the Children of Ireland from Being a Burden to Their Parents or Country" may be the most widely anthologized essay in the English language.

(See **Italics**.)

Note: When using quotation marks, be sure to place other marks of punctuation correctly.

The rule is simple. Periods and commas always go *inside* the quotation marks. Colons, dashes, and semicolons always go *outside* the quotation marks. Exclamation points and question marks go inside the quotation marks if they are part of the quoted material; otherwise, they go outside the quotation marks:

Period

For tomorrow, read James Lynn Barton's poem "To a Lady in My Arms."

Comma

For tomorrow, read "To a Lady in My Arms," which was written by James Lynn Barton in 1967.

Colon

For tomorrow, read "To a Lady in My Arms": it provides a perfect antidote to the genteel, squeamish gloom of "The Love Song of J. Alfred Prufrock."

Dash

For tomorrow, read "To a Lady in My Arms"—by James Lynn Barton—and come prepared to contrast it with "The Love Song of J. Alfred Prufrock."

Semicolon

For tomorrow, read "To a Lady in My Arms"; we will compare and contrast it with "The Love Song of J. Alfred Prufrock."

Exclamation Point

He shouted, "Bizarre!"

I can't *stand* "To a Lady in My Arms"!

Question Mark

Have you read "To a Lady in My Arms"?

We are going to discuss the question "Is there life after death?"

Note also: for a quotation within a quotation, use an "inverted comma" for a "single" quotation mark (') as opposed to a "double" quotation mark ("):

"The smell down below was as unexpected as it was frightful. One would have thought hundreds of paraffin lamps had been flaring and smoking in that hole for days. The man with me coughed and said, 'Funny smell, sir.' I answered negligently, 'It's good for the health, they say,' and walked aft."

—Joseph Conrad, "Youth"

ref **Reference (of pronouns)**—In general, use no pronoun that lacks a definite antecedent.

1.   Each pronoun should point clearly to its antecedent (the noun it replaces); the reference should never be vague and indefinite:

ORIGINAL

At the store I was told *they* were out of French bread and mushrooms. (*They* has no antecedent; it refers vaguely to the proprietors of the store.)

In the morning paper *it* said that the killer of six coeds had been captured. (*It* has no definite antecedent.)

REVISION

At the store I was told by the clerk that *he* was out of French bread and mushrooms. (*He* clearly refers back to its antecedent, *clerk*.)

A story in the morning paper said that the killer of six coeds had been captured. (The pronoun *it* has been replaced by the noun *story*.)

2.   Do not use a pronoun to refer to an entire preceding sentence, clause, or phrase:

ORIGINAL

Finance charges usually add
hundreds of dollars to the
purchase price of a car. *This*
should be taken into
consideration in computing the
total cost. (*This* refers vaguely to
the idea expressed in the entire
first sentence.)

REVISION

Finance charges usually add
hundreds of dollars to the
purchase price of a car. This *fact*
should be taken into
consideration in computing the
total cost. (*This* is now used as a
demonstrative adjective
modifying *fact*.)

3.   Avoid ambiguous pronoun reference:

Ambiguous pronoun reference occurs when a pronoun
might refer to any of several persons or things. When the
reference is ambiguous, the entire sentence needs to be
rewritten to make the reference clear.

ORIGINAL

Bob told John *he* needed to get *his*
hair cut. After all, Martha and
Judy were going to the dance too,
and *their* appearance was
important. (Who needed a haircut,
Bob or John? Whose appearance
was important? The antecedents
of *he*, *his*, and *their* are
ambiguous.)

REVISION

Bob told John, "*I* need to get *my*
hair cut. After all, Martha and
Judy are going to the dance too,
and *our* appearance is important."
(*I* and *my* clearly refer to Bob. *Our*
clearly refers to Bob and John. The
pronoun reference is no longer
ambiguous.)

(See **Shift/Point of View.**)

rep **Repetition**—Do not thoughtlessly repeat sounds, words, ideas, or sentence patterns.

Many kinds of repetition make artful, effective writing, especially when the writer uses repetition with some conscious aim in mind. Thus alliteration—the repetition of initial sounds of words—is a poetic device occasionally used in writing prose. The repetition of important words establishes continuity, coherence, and unity. The repetition of ideas can emphasize an important point. But thoughtless repetition of sounds, words, sentence patterns, or ideas stands out like crumbs on a beard.

In the following examples notice the differences between thoughtful, effective repetition and careless, ineffective repetition:

Sounds

EFFECTIVE: Our country right or wrong. When right to be kept right; when wrong to be put right. (Carl Schurz)

CARELESS: A part of my heart loved her, but my mind was blind to her charms, even when I held her in my arms and stared at the swarms of golden specks to be seen deep in her green eyes. (Rhyme, we can probably agree, makes prose sound like bad verse.)

Words

EFFECTIVE: *Persons attempting* to find a motive in this narrative will be prosecuted; *persons attempting* to find a moral in it will be banished; *persons attempting* to find a plot in it will be shot. (Mark Twain)

CARELESS: Next would be growth. It is hard to say that this could be called a *reality* of life, but one must admit that it is *real.* This is an easy *reality* to *realize.* (We are not sure what this means. But the repetition makes it sound sillier and emptier than it *really* is.)

Sentence Patterns

EFFECTIVE: It is said an Eastern monarch once charged his wise men to invent him a sentence to be ever in view, and which should be true and appropriate in all times and situations. They presented him the words: "And this, too, shall pass away." *How much it expresses! How chastening in the hour of pride! How consoling in the depths of affliction!* (Abraham Lincoln)

CARELESS: The cat walked along a branch. The dog sat under the tree. I stood on the sidewalk. I wondered what would happen next. (Do not make every sentence a brief, staccato statement, beginning with the subject and verb, unless you are seeking a

particular effect. Vary your sentence structure
slightly.)

Ideas

EFFECTIVE: It was very pleasant to me to get a letter from
you the other day. Perhaps I should have found it
pleasanter if I had been able to decipher it. I don't
think I mastered anything beyond the date (which I
knew) and the signature (which I guessed at). There's
a singular and perpetual charm in a letter of yours; it
never grows old, it never loses its novelty. . . . Other
letters are read and thrown away and forgotten, but
yours are kept forever—unread. One of them will last
a reasonable man a lifetime. (Thomas Bailey Aldrich)

CARELESS: Thurber's essay is one of entertainment for
his readers, also giving vent to his pet peeves. That is
just exactly what it is, pure enjoyment to read in a
satirical fashion. It is an entertaining essay about the
life of a typical college student. Actually, this subject
is a difficult one to write about. . . . (Yes, indeed. This
student has nothing to say on the assigned subject, so
he says it three times—in the hope that verbosity will
resemble substance—before he admits that he has
nothing to say.)

(See **Sentence Structure/Style.**)

Run-Together Sentences—Do not write two or more
independent clauses as one sentence.   **rt**

> There are three cars in my garage none of them is very
> new.

This statement is a run-together sentence (also known as a
run-on or *fused* sentence) because it consists of two
separate main clauses joined without appropriate
punctuation or conjunctions. Closer examination shows
that the run-together sentence is really two sentences:

> There are three cars in my garage. None of them is very
> new.

You may correct run-together sentences in any of
several ways—but do *not* make the correction at random.
Think intelligently about it. The way you choose should
depend on the sentences themselves, the rhythms you feel
are appropriate, and the context of the surrounding
sentences.

1.   Correct some run-together sentences by separating the
main clauses with a period.

(See Period.)

ORIGINAL

I love Sue however it is unlikely I will marry her. (*I love Sue* is a main clause. It should be set off from the other main clause.)

REVISION

I love Sue. However, it is unlikely I will marry her.

2. Correct some run-together sentences by separating the main clauses with a semicolon.

(See **Semicolon.**)

ORIGINAL

I like to look at the mountains they are very beautiful at this time of the year. (*I like to look at the mountains* is a main clause. It should be set off from the other main clause.)

REVISION

I like to look at the mountains; they are very beautiful at this time of the year.

3. Correct some run-together sentences by joining the main clauses with a comma and a coordinating conjunction (*and, or, nor, but, yet, for*).

(See **Comma.**)

ORIGINAL

The morning was golden their spirits were high. (*The morning*

REVISION

The morning was golden, and their spirits were high.

was golden is a main clause. It
should be set off from the other
main clause.)

4.   Correct some run-together sentences by subordinating
one clause and using appropriate comma punctuation.

(See **Comma** and **Subordination.**)

ORIGINAL

I like to work in the sun I have to
be very careful not to get
sunburned, however. (*I like to
work in the sun* is a main clause. It
should be set off from the other
main clause.)

REVISION

Although I like to work in the sun,
I have to be very careful not to get
sunburned. (The main clause *I
like to work in the sun* has been
subordinated—that is, linked to
the other main clause by a
subordinate conjunction,
although—and set off by comma
punctuation.)

semi

Semicolon—Use the semicolon to separate two or more closely related independent clauses not joined by a coordinating conjunction; use the semicolon for rhetorical effect; use the semicolon, as required, to prevent confusion.

1.   Use the semicolon to separate two or more closely related independent clauses not joined by a coordinating conjunction:

> Claire stirred the jam; I sterilized the Mason jars.

> The cat leaped into my arms; the raccoon, puzzled, stared curiously at us both.

Note:
(a)   The coordinating conjunctions in English are *and, or, nor, but, yet,* and *for.*
(b)   The semicolon in the construction may be replaced by a comma plus a coordinating conjunction or a period with a new sentence.

Claire stirred the jam, *and* I sterilized the Mason jars.

Claire stirred the jam. I sterilized the Mason jars.

(c)   In a long, complicated sentence, the semicolon may also be used *with* a coordinating conjunction:

Sometimes, after long hours of writhing in pain and loneliness, she felt like putting an end to it all; *but* then she remembered Bob and clung tenaciously to her hope, for she knew that no matter what, he loved her, even though he had kicked out all her teeth.

(d)   The semicolon is most frequently used to join two main clauses connected rhetorically by a conjunctive adverb. (Conjunctive adverbs are words like *however, nevertheless, consequently, then, thereupon, moreover, therefore, hence, furthermore, besides.* They show transitions in thought, but they do not link clauses grammatically. See **Comma Splice.**)

Ted slept on the floor; *however,* she retired to the roof.

The cat leaped into my arms; *then* the raccoon, puzzled, stared curiously at us both.

Note, first, that the conjunctive adverb is generally set off by a comma; and, second, that the conjunctive adverb (unlike true conjunctions) can be readily moved to other positions in the clause:

Ted slept on the floor; she, *however*, retired to the roof.

Ted slept on the floor; she retired to the roof, *however*.

2. Use the semicolon for rhetorical effect:

Occasionally the semicolon can be used with great effectiveness to link together a series of short main clauses:

A quarter moon is still up; the eastern sky is pink behind the rim of mountains; but black clouds lie on them to the south, and the morning is still dark over the lights of Redwood City; birds sing; down in the park, a lone rooster crows; sunrise comes to my silent room, atop my little hill; it is now 5:10 A.M.

3. Use the semicolon to prevent confusion in constructions which, like the following, require internal comma punctuation:

In Paris that year I knew Martha St. John, who wrote dirty poetry and got filthy drunk on two glasses of wine; Jonathan Wild, who was later arrested for attacking the Eiffel Tower with a war-surplus bazooka, screaming, "I'll get you, you bloody Martians!"; and Gilmore Stern, an apoplectic young painter who lived in a huge, drafty studio with two scrawny models and a pack of greyhounds.

Note: always place the semicolon *after* a quotation mark:

> I enjoyed Hemingway's "A Clean Well-Lighted Place";
> that's more than I can say for his "Big Two-Hearted
> River."

Sentence Structure/Style—Make each sentence as
effective as possible in its context; prefer the plain style.

SS

One learns to write well by writing and rewriting so
diligently and carefully that the fitting word, the just
construction, the perfectly appropriate rhythm comes
with its own polished, natural eloquence. To a very few
writers such strength and ease require only the effort of
lifting a pen or flicking graceful fingers over the keys of a
singing typewriter. Most of us, however, must work at
writing—work hard, with little advice, or no advice, or
bad advice, which is unspeakably worse than no advice.
And as your writing matures, you'll probably discover for
yourself that most of the advice you've been given was bad
advice, given by people who either don't write at all or
write badly, and hence compounded of ignorance,
prejudice, and mindless devotion to tradition, qualities
molded by obstinacy and confusion into a set of *Rules for
Writing Well*. Forget it. Most of what you've been taught
under that rubric is tainted: it is unadulterated rubbish.

1. Correcting faulty sentence structure (see **Awkward Phrasing**):

When a sentence goes astray—and comes back marked SS for *Sentence structure/Style*—you can only try to improve it by rewriting it. Make it *sound* correct, using your natural sentence sense as you cut and add words, shift phrases and clauses. No set of rules can tell you exactly what to do, since each bad sentence is bad in its own special way; it bears the stench of corrupt individuality; and it must be cleaned and polished to an immaculate uniqueness. For example:

ORIGINAL

I like the beach because of its clean, salty air, its fine sand, and it has a variety of various outdoor activities available. (*Various* following *variety* is awkward and unnecessary. The second clause would be better expressed as a third parallel phrase.)

Johnny Cash, one of America's greatest Western musicians, and who is extremely popular among young people because of his political and social sympathies, is a great live performer, one who

REVISION

I like the beach because of its clean, salty air, its fine sand, and the variety of outdoor activities available there.

Johnny Cash, a great Western musician who is extremely popular among young people because of his political and social views, is an excellent live performer, able to charm and can charm and thrill any audience. (The first *and* does not belong in this sentence; *sympathies* is not quite the right word; *greatest* followed by *great* makes awkward repetition; the two appositive constructions introduced by *one* and the two adjective clauses introduced by *who* are extremely awkward as they are yoked together in this sentence.)

thrill any audience. (The sentence is still perhaps too long: the idea expressed by the adjective clause probably needs to be developed and emphasized in a separate sentence.)

2.   Improving your sentence structure:

As Socrates said, "Agree with me if I seem to speak the truth." There *are* devices of style that you can use systematically to improve the sentence structure of everything you write, from love letters to essay examinations. We offer this brief discussion of such devices, however, not as a set of rules but as a series of suggestions; you may either accept or reject them. George Orwell, in "Politics and the English Language," has stated the basic principle: "If you simplify your English, you are freed from the worst follies of orthodoxy."

(a)   *Prefer the short sentence to the long.*

That is not to say that you should write in a

"Dick-and-Jane" style, but that short sentences are direct, powerful, and easy to write. They have strength and force. They have the natural dignity of the spoken language. And they are much more readable.

(b)   *Vary the length of your sentences.*

An objection to short sentences is that they are dull, flat, and choppy. But only when used carelessly. There are two answers to this objection, then: *first,* turn some of your short sentences into longer ones by joining the main clauses with proper punctuation—semicolons, colons, and dashes—so that your sentences *seem* longer, even though most of your ideas are still stated in brief main clauses; *second,* achieve the effect of variation by writing some extremely short sentences and some rather long ones. Shift rhythms. The result will not be dull, flat, choppy sentences, but zestful, pungent, cadenced prose.

(c)   *Begin most sentences with the subject and the verb.*

The natural sentence in English today is the "cumulative" sentence, which (like this one) begins with the subject and verb of the main clause and adds modifying clauses and phrases if necessary, so that ideas "accumulate" to cling to the main statement. An occasional subordinate clause, prepositional phrase, or participial construction at the beginning of a sentence does no harm; in fact, judiciously used, it may even interject a spirited, unanticipated shift in rhythm, improving the movement of an entire passage.

But *do not* use such constructions very often: you'll send your readers bouncing through a clatter of variation—of gerunds, gerundives, participles, noun and adverb clauses, prepositional phrases—until their heads spin and their teeth ache.

Elegant variation, as it is usually taught, will *poison* your style.

(d)   *Use a familiar vocabulary.*

Let us quote H. W. Fowler in *The King's English:*

> Anyone who wishes to become a good writer should endeavor, before he allows himself to be tempted by the more showy qualities, to be direct, simple, brief, vigorous, and lucid. This general principle may be translated into practical rules in the domain of vocabulary as follows:—
> Prefer the familiar word to the farfetched.
> Prefer the concrete word to the abstract.
> Prefer the single word to the circumlocution.
> Prefer the short word to the long.
> Prefer the Saxon word to the Romance.
>
> These rules are given roughly in the order of merit; the last is also the least.

In giving similar advice in "Politics and the English Language," George Orwell aptly sums up for us this discussion of sentence structure and style:

(i) Never use a metaphor, simile, or other figure of speech which you are used to seeing in print.

(ii) Never use a long word where a short one will do.

(iii) If it is possible to cut a word out, always cut it out.

(iv) Never use the passive voice where you can use the active.

(v) Never use a foreign phrase, a scientific word, or a jargon word if you think of an everyday English equivalent.

(vi) Break any of these rules sooner than say anything outright barbarous.

(See **Awkward Phrasing, Subordination,** and **Wrong Word.**)

---

shf/pv   **Shift/Point of View**—Do not shift carelessly from one point of view to another: use one pronoun consistently in order to maintain a single point of view.

ORIGINAL	REVISION
I like to get up very early when *I* am forced to write something. *You*	*I* like to get up very early when *I* am forced to write something. *I*

can think most clearly in the morning, and the earlier *I* get up, the more *I* get accomplished. (The writer should not shift from *I* to *you*: he or she should maintain one point of view consistently.)

can think most clearly early in the morning, and the earlier *I* get up, the more *I* get accomplished.

Students must prepare for *their* final exams. *You* will not get far without adequate preparation. (*You*, the second person pronoun, is carelessly used here to refer to the third person plural pronoun, *their*, which in turn refers back to *students*.)

Students must prepare for *their* final exams. *They* will not get far without adequate preparation. (The third person plural pronouns *their* and *they* now are used correctly to refer to *students*.)

(See **Reference.**)

Shift/Tense—Stick consistently to one verb tense (the form that indicates time). Do not change tenses unnecessarily.

shf/t

   In telling a story, writing an anecdote, or summarizing a writer's argument, use one verb tense consistently. For plot summaries in particular, use the *present tense*; the convention for doing so is firmly established.

ORIGINAL

In Sophocles' *Oedipus Rex*, Oedipus *learns* that he *has killed* his father and *married* his mother, Jocasta. When he *found* this out, he *tore* a pin from Jocasta's dress—after she *had hanged* herself—and *stabbed* out his eyes. At the end of the play, he *walks* away blind, banished from his kingdom. (In the first and third sentences, the writer uses the present and present perfect tenses. In the second sentence, however, he shifts to the past and past perfect tenses, thereby distorting the time-angle from which he views events.)

REVISION

In Sophocles' *Oedipus Rex*, Oedipus *learns* that he *has killed* his father and *married* his mother, Jocasta. When he *finds* this out, he *tears* a pin from Jocasta's dress—after she *has hanged* herself—and *stabs* out his eyes. At the end of the play, he *walks* away blind, banished from his kingdom. (Now the present and present perfect tenses are used consistently. Note that the present perfect tense—as in *has hanged*—is used for past events as they are viewed from the present.)

(See **Tense.**)

---

sp

Spelling—Spell each word correctly. Carefully correct every error in spelling. Learn the basic rules of English orthography (correct spelling), and master a list of frequently misspelled words.

Although poor spellers seldom fail to communicate their meaning clearly, they may alarm and annoy their reader, creating a mistrust so keen that the reader rejects the writers' perceptions and ideas along with their misspellings.

Certain good habits characterize the work of good spellers. Good spellers consult a dictionary for the correct spelling of every doubtful word. No experience, no rules can take the place of a recent college desk dictionary. Good spellers also use their memory-system—eyes, ears, hands—in studying the spelling of a difficult word: they *look* at the word and note its syllabification; they *pronounce* the word so that they *hear* it with fidelity; they *write* it more than once to mark its shape in the muscles and nerves of their hands. Their practice is to look, hear, write.

Besides using a dictionary, good spellers know a few basic rules of spelling—and are familiar with many of the exceptions to the rules.

English orthography by its very nature admits many exceptions. Before learning any rules, then, you should thoughtfully consider some of the factors that are responsible for the difficulties of English spelling. First, the dissemination of printed books, beginning about 1500, tended to fix the spelling of English words even though their pronunciation continued to change. In the word *knight,* for instance, the silent *k* and *gh* were once pronounced. Second, English vocabulary is made up of a high percentage of foreign words, and their etymology tends to influence their spelling. Third, our alphabet of twenty-six letters is simply inadequate to represent systematically the twenty-one vowel sounds and twenty-five consonant sounds of twentieth-century American English. Finally, as Mario Pei points out in *The Story of English* (New York: Fawcett World Library, 1952, pp. 280–81), a tremendous variety of letters may be used to represent a single sound—there are fourteen possible ways to spell the *sh* sound—or, conversely, we may get a number of different sounds out of one combination of letters, such as the seven different sounds represented by *ough* (dough, bought, bough, rough, through, thorough, and hiccough). In short, as Pei says, "English spelling is the world's most awesome mess" (p. 280).

Spelling Rules

To eliminate some of the difficulties of English spelling, you should learn the following five rules, which are regular enough to be useful:

1. *Doubling the final consonant.* When a word ends with a single consonant preceded by a single vowel, *double* the final consonant before a suffix beginning with a vowel if the base word has only one syllable, or if the base word is accented on the last syllable.

Note the three elements in this complex rule:

(a)   The base word must end with a single consonant preceded by a single vowel, as in *begin, stop, occur, prefer.*

(b)   The base word must have only one syllable or be accented on the final syllable, as in *big, drop,* and *brag,* or in deFER, exPEL, and reFER.

(c)   The suffix must begin with a vowel, as in *-ar, -er, -ess, -ed,* and *-ing.*

Examples (base word + consonant + suffix):

adMIT	+	t	+	ed	=	adMITTed
beGIN	+	n	+	ing	=	beGINNing
comPEL	+	l	+	ing	=	comPELLing
deFER	+	r	+	ed	=	deFERRed
fog	+	g	+	y	=	foGGy
stop	+	p	+	ed	=	stoPPed

Note: Do not double the final consonant if it is preceded by more than one vowel: *appear, appeared, appearance.* Do not double the final consonant in words ending in silent *e: write, writing; come, coming; dine, dining.* (An obvious exception is *write, written:* in *written* the spelling changes to accommodate the change in pronunciation, as the long *i* of *write* becomes the short *i* of *written.*)

2. *I before e.* When the sound is *ee,* write *i* before *e* except after *c;* otherwise write *e* before *i.* A useful mnemonic (memory) device is the rhyme

> Write *i* before *e*
> Except after *c,*
> Or if sounded like *a*
> As in *neighbor* or *weigh.*

Examples
(*i* before *e*
except after *c*)   (after *c*)   (sounded like *a*)

belief	perceive	veil
grief	ceiling	reign
pierce	receive	freight
yield	receipt	vein

Exceptions: *either, neither, weird, forfeit, leisure, seize, species, height, foreign.*

3. *Dropping the silent e.* When a word ends in a silent *e,* drop the *e* when you add a suffix beginning with a vowel; keep the *e* when you add a suffix beginning with a consonant.

Examples (suffix beginning with a vowel):

| admire | + | able | = | admirable |
| bite | + | ing | = | biting |

create	+	ive	=	creative
fame	+	ous	=	famous
mange	+	y	=	mangy

Exceptions: words ending in *ce* or *ge* usually retain the *e* to preserve a soft *c* or *g* sound, as in *advantageous*, *changeable*, *outrageous*, and *noticeable*. Variant spellings are also possible—and equally correct: movable, moveable; likable, likeable; lovable, loveable.

Examples (suffix beginning with a consonant):

care	+	ful	=	careful
life	+	like	=	lifelike
advertise	+	ment	=	advertisement
complete	+	ly	=	completely

Exceptions: *wholly, argument, judgment, truly, awful.*

4.   *Changing y to i.* When a word ends with a consonant + *y*, change the *y* to *i* when you add a suffix. Usually do not change the *y* if the suffix begins with *i*.

Examples (consonant + *y* + suffix):

baby	+	es	=	babies
baby	+	ing	=	babying
				(suffix begins with *i*)
busy	+	ly	=	busily

defy	+	ance	=	defiance
forty	+	eth	=	fortieth
happy	+	er	=	happier
lobby	+	ed	=	lobbied
likely	+	hood	=	likelihood
marry	+	age	=	marriage
weary	+	ness	=	weariness

Exceptions: *dryly, dryness; shyly, shyness; slyly, slyness; wryly, wryness.*

Note: When the final *y* is preceded by a vowel instead of a consonant, do not change the *y* to *i*, as in *buy, buyer; employ, employment; play, played.*
   Exceptions: *daily, gaiety, paid, said.*

5.   *Adding prefixes.* Do not change the basic spelling of a word when you add prefixes such as *un-, mis-,* or *dis-.*
   Examples:

   discharge

   disenchanted

   misspell

   misunderstood

unhappy

unnecessary

Spelling List

The following words are frequently misspelled by college students.* When you have mastered these words, you will have eliminated many of your personal spelling difficulties.

accept	arguing	believe
achieve	argument	beneficial
acquire	arithmetic	benefited
adolescence	article	Britain
advice	athlete	business
advise	attendance	capital
all right	author	category
analysis	basically	choose
analyze	beginner	chose
apparent	beginning	clothes
appearance	belief	coming

*Based on a study of spelling by college students made by Thomas Clark Pollock ("Spelling Report," *College English*, November 1954).

comparative

conceive

conscience

conscious

consider

consistent

controversial

criticism

criticize

curriculum

dealt

decide

definite

definition

dependent

describe

description

despair

disastrous

disease

effect

embarrass

environment

equipped

exaggerate

excellent

except

existence

fallacy

foreign

forty

friend

fulfill

government

grammar

guarantee

guidance

hear

height

here

heroes

heroine

hypocrisy

independent

influential

intelligent

interest

its (possessive pronoun)

it's (contraction = it is)

laid

led

leisure

lives

lonely

loose

lose

maintenance

mathematics

mere

mischief

necessary

Negroes

ninety

noticeable

noticing

obstacle

occasion

occurred

occurrence

opinion

opponent

optimism

origin

paid

parallel

particular

passed

past

performance

permanent

personal

personnel

persuade

piece

possess

possession

possible

practical

precede

preferred

prejudice

prepare

prevalent

principal

principle

privilege

probably

procedure

proceed

professor

psychology

pursue

quantity

quiet

quite

realize

receive

recommend

referring

relieve

repetition

rhyme (variant: rime)

rhythm

rising

sacrifice

seize

sense

separate

sergeant

shepherd

similar

sophomore

speech

subtle

success

surprise

temperament

than

their

themselves

then

there

therefore

they're

to

too

tragedy

tries

two

vacuum

villain

weather

weird

where

whether

whole

who's (contraction = who is)

whose (possessive pronoun)

woman

write

writer

writing

written

yield

your (possessive pronoun)

you're (contraction = you are)

Subordination—Subordinate less important ideas by   **sub**
placing them in dependent clauses clearly related to the
main clause or clauses of the sentence.

Since some ideas are much more important than others,
you will want to emphasize those ideas by stating them in
main clauses. But such emphasis is difficult to achieve if
you express *every* idea in consecutive main clauses or
coordinate clauses. To emphasize important ideas, then,
and at the same time to convey proper relationships
between ideas, *subordinate* less important ideas by
placing them in dependent clauses or in phrases, or by
expressing them as one word if possible.

1.   Subordinate (dependent) clauses

ORIGINAL

The sun on the white snow was
brilliant. I had to shade my eyes.
(Each idea receives the same
emphasis; that is, each is placed
in a main clause. No relationship
of ideas is conveyed.)

REVISION

*Because the sun on the white
snow was brilliant,* I had to shade
my eyes. (The idea in the first
clause is now subordinate: it has
been placed in a dependent clause
introduced by *because.* In
addition to shifting the emphasis
to the second clause, the new
arrangement establishes a
cause-and-effect relationship.)

Coach Wilson expects to have a winning team this season. She is in her second year. (Neither idea receives proper emphasis, and no significant relationship is fixed between the two ideas.)

Coach Wilson, *who is in her second year,* expects to have a winning team this season. (The second sentence, now a nonrestrictive adjective clause, is properly subordinated to the first, since it merely adds some extra information.)

2.   Phrases

ORIGINAL

He was failing in his classes. He was fatigued. He had been working forty hours a week at his job. He decided to quit school. (The short, choppy sentences give emphasis to none of the ideas.)

REVISION

Failing his classes and fatigued from working forty hours a week at his job, he decided to quit school. (The subordinate ideas are expressed as phrases, while the most important idea is stated in the main clause.)

3.   Words

ORIGINAL

Her eyes were tired, and they were in need of cold compresses.

REVISION

Her *tired* eyes were in need of cold compresses. (The first clause is replaced by the adjective *tired.*)

Tense—Make the tense of each verb agree with the time of the action. Do not carelessly shift from one tense to another.

1. Use the correct tense for each verb:

    He *directs* the company. (present tense)

    He *directed* the company. (past tense)

    He *will direct* the company. (future tense)

2. Shift verb tense only when the time of the action shifts:

    She *borrowed* the money and *bought* new equipment. (The time of the action does not shift; thus the verbs are both in the simple past tense.)

    Because she *increased* production last fall, she *is leading* all of her competitors. (The action in the subordinate clause is prior to the action of the main clause. There actually *is* a shift in the time of action from past to present. Thus the shift from the past tense *increased* to the present tense *is leading* is correct and proper.)

Note: For further discussion of shifts in the tense of verbs, see **Shift/Tense.**

3. Use the present tense for something that is always so:

Many travelers have said that San Francisco *is* a city of breathtaking beauty. (*Is*, not *was*.)

---

ti

Titles—Make your titles relevant and interesting.

Your titles should be relevant to the subject of your essay, obviously; most titles are. But your title should also be interesting; most titles aren't.

Some titles, of course, are entirely functional: they name subjects. We'll read on if the subjects interest us. "The Mystery Story," "Hypnotism Today," "The Facts about Solar Living"—the titles attract us if we fancy the subject.

A good title is a lure. And finding one requires only a little thought about a few suggestions:

1.   *Ask an intriguing question.* A question has the advantage, also, of suggesting both a beginning and an ending for your essay. Examples: "Was the World Made for Man?" (Mark Twain); "Why Should the Majority Rule?" (Walter Lippmann); "Is Everybody Happy?" (John Ciardi).

2.   *Use the First Person.* Invite your reader to share your ideas; you'll seem direct and plausible. Examples: "Why I Write" (George Orwell); "Why I Want a Wife" (Judy Syfers); "Why I Am an Agnostic" (Clarence Darrow).

3.   *Use alliteration.* Alliteration is the repetition of initial sounds in successive words; it has a lively lilt; it's memorable. Examples: "Getting More Go from Your Gas" (Robert Sikorsky); "Perils of a Procrastinator" (Will Stanton); "Diet and Die" (Karen Marblestone).

4.   *Try controversy.* Attack a sacred institution; arouse anger or doubt: you won't be ignored. Examples: "The Myth of the Declaration [of Independence]" (Garry Wills); "Our Image of God Must Go" (John A. T. Robinson); "Women Are Prisoners of Their Sex" (Brigid Brophy).

5.   *Give advice.* We thrive on curiosity; make the best of our need. Examples: "If at First You Don't Succeed, Quit" (Steven Cahn); "How to Get Thin and *Stay* Thin"

(*Reader's Digest*); "How to be Bratty and Drive Your Sister Batty" (Delia Ephron).

Many of these titles, of course, fit more than one category (sixty percent are alliterative). Phrases, single sentences, and quotations (especially bits of dialogue) make good titles: "Thinking as a Hobby" (William Golding); "You *Can* Help Your Children Learn" (Maya Pines); "I Can't Hold on Anymore!" (Warren Young).

In fact, if you use your imagination, you'll find good titles lurking just at the edge of consciousness. Work at them—and suddenly "Wild Wyoming" will pop up to displace "What I Did Last Summer."

Note: follow standard editorial practice in the treatment of titles. These rules will cover most situations:

1.   Center the title of your own paper in capital letters. If you have a separate title page, center your title in capital letters halfway down the page:

PUMPING IRON

On the first page of your essay, drop down about one-third of the page and center your title and name thus:

PUMPING IRON
by
Alice Little

Note: Your instructor may require that you place your name elsewhere, such as in the upper right-hand corner along with the date and course number.

2.   Place the titles of shorter works, when you name them, in quotation marks. When you refer to the title of an essay, story, or poem, or any part of a longer work, place the title in quotation marks:

> In Susan Glaspell's story "A Jury of Her Peers," there is an ironic reversal in the roles of men and women.

(See **Quotation Marks.**)

3.   Italicize the titles of any longer works when you refer to them. Italicize (underline) the titles of novels, plays, books or nonfiction, movies, and television programs:

> *The Great Gatsby* deals with the American Dream.
>
> *Hamlet* is one of the world's best-known plays.
>
> Have you seen *Citizen Kane*?

(See **Italics.**)

Topic Sentence—Use the topic sentence to state the main idea of your paragraph.

ts

A topic sentence does two things: first, it lays down your subject; second, it puts forth your main idea about that subject. We can say, then, that a topic sentence has two parts: a *subject*; and something said about that subject, which we can call the *focus*. For example:

SUBJECT	FOCUS
editing	. . . is very important
ice cream	I like . . .
music	. . . is interesting and enjoyable

A good topic sentence has a *limited* subject and a *sharp* focus. A limited subject clearly marks off your specific material; a sharp focus points out *exactly* what you will say about that material. A weak topic sentence, by contrast, has a broad subject and a vague focus; such a sentence leads nowhere in particular—except to a loose, poorly unified, badly developed, disorganized paragraph.

ORIGINAL	REVISION
Editing is very important to the written word. (This topic sentence has a broad subject—editing—and a vague focus.)	Editing is a "glamour" career sought by many English majors. (This topic sentence represents an improvement because the subject is limited to editing as a career and the focus is sharper.)

Copy editing requires a knowledge of correct grammar and usage, an eye for good organization, and an ear for pleasing style. (This topic sentence is better still because the subject is more limited and the focus is much sharper. The writer has now committed herself to writing about *copy editing* instead of about editing generally, and she must show that copy editing involves very specific abilities: *a knowledge of correct grammar and usage, an eye for good organization, and an ear for pleasing style.*)

Music is interesting and enjoyable.

Dixieland jazz combines a feeling for familiar rhythms and an ability to improvise.

Transitions—Use transitional devices to show your reader how your ideas fit together—that is, to help you achieve continuity in your writing.   tr

Transitions are like bridges: they carry your reader across the gaps between sentences and paragraphs. Find the meaning in the etymology: *trans*, "across"; *-ition*, "going"; *trans-ition*—"going across." So a *transition* is a word or a phrase that connects ideas. Within the paragraph, transitions show how sentences are tied to each other and to the main idea.

Learn to use three common transitional devices:

1. Pronoun reference
2. Repetition of important words
3. Transitional expressions

1. First, learn to use pronoun reference to achieve continuity:

Take the following paragraph as an example of the way pronouns can be used to tie sentences together in the paragraph. Here, Don Fabun begins with the topic sentence "We live, for the most part, in little boxes." In the rest of the paragraph Fabun gets continuity by using the word *they* to refer back to *boxes*. Note that the pronoun appears at or near the beginning of most of the sentences, and that there is never any doubt about what word the pronoun refers back to:

We live, for the most part, in little boxes. *They* may be clustered together, as in office buildings or apartment

houses or hotels, or *they* may be scattered over the
countryside as in tract housing. But *they* are still little
boxes. As forms for habitation, *they* are relics of
another age.

> —Don Fabun, *Dimensions of Change*
> (Encino, Ca.: Glencoe, 1971, p. 61)

2.   Second, learn to repeat important words to achieve
continuity:

In one shining paragraph from his essay "The Culture of
Machine Living," Max Lerner gets continuity by repeating
the word *standardized* (as well as by using clear pronoun
reference). He has placed his topic sentence at the end of
the preceding paragraph: "Someone with a satiric intent
could do a withering take-off on the rituals of American
standardization." Now, he writes:

Most American babies . . . are born in *standardized*
hospitals, with a *standardized* tag put around them to
keep them from getting confused with other
standardized products of the hospital. Many of them
grow up in uniform rows of tenements or suburban
houses. They are wheeled about in *standard*
perambulators, shiny or shabby as may be, fed from
standardized bottles with *standardized* nipples
according to *standardized* formulas, and tied up with
standardized diapers. In childhood they are fed

standardized breakfast foods out of *standardized* boxes with pictures of *standardized* heroes on them. They are sent to monotonously similar schoolhouses, where almost uniformly *standardized* teachers ladle out to them *standardized* information out of *standardized* textbooks. . . .

—Max Lerner, "The Culture of Machine Living," *America as a Civilization* (New York: Simon & Schuster, 1957)

But that is, after all, a *tour de force,* a highly polished display of technical virtuosity—and you are not very likely to want to imitate its methods. For a more practical example of the way word repetition can be used to tie sentences together, look closely at this paragraph: it gets continuity by repeating the word *smoke:*

The pioneer American farmer had his small *smoke* rooms or *smoke* ovens connected to the fireplaces and chimneys within his dwelling—from the cellar to the attic. Often they were on the second floor between two upper bedrooms. The attic *smoke* chamber did the best job, though, for there meat could be *smoked* with the least amount of heat. Meat was difficult to keep in those days, and *smoking* was more a preserving than a flavoring operation. In the 1700s, when the *smoke* ovens first went outdoors to become part of the barn complex, they often were large enough for a person to enter and hence were called *smokehouses*.

—Eric Sloane, *An Age of Barns*
(Funk & Wagnalls, 1967, p. 84)

3.   Finally, learn to use transitional expressions to achieve continuity:

Transitional expressions are words and phrases that, for the most part, have only one job in the language: to show how events or ideas or things are related to one another. Alone, they mean nothing: they are empty words. Suppose someone walks up to you and says, "In the first place, however, thus, consequently, nevertheless, last!" See?

But as gimmicks and gadgets of language they are most useful. They underline infinitely important relationships; they give you an extraordinarily exact way of showing how sentences in a paragraph are related to the main idea and to each other.

Pull the transitional expressions from this paragraph, for example—and see how little sense is left:

Result: introduces conclusion drawn from preceding paragraphs

Addition: shows how one thing happens after another

Addition: introduces further explanation

Result: introduces conclusion drawn from details in this paragraph

Contrast: introduces contrasting conclusion

Addition: introduces explanation for preceding statement

Addition: introduces further explanation

Thus, in the perspective of biology, war first dwindles to the status of a rare curiosity. Further probing, however, makes it loom larger again. For one thing, it is a form of intra-specific struggle, and as such may be useless or even harmful to the species as a whole. Then we find that one of the very few animal species that make war is man; and man is today not merely the highest product of evolution, but the only type still capable of real evolutionary progress. And, war, though it need not always be so harmful to the human species and its progress, indubitably is so when conducted in the total fashion which is necessary in this technological age. Thus war is not merely a human problem; it is a biological problem of the broadest scope, for on its abolition may depend life's ability to continue the progress which it has slowly but steadily achieved through more than a thousand million years.

—Sir Julian Huxley, "War as a Biological Phenomenon" from *On Living in a Revolution* (New York: Harper & Row, 1942)

As you write, then, keep before you this "catalog" of transitional expressions, organized around the relationships they usually bring out:

Addition

additionally, again, also, and also, and then, as well, besides, beyond that, equally important, first (second, third, fourth, finally, last, etc.), for one thing, further, furthermore, in addition, likewise, moreover, next, now, on top of that, over and above that

Comparison

in the same way, likewise, similarly

Contrast

after all, although this may be true, and yet, be that as it may, but, even so, for all that, however, in contrast, in other circumstances, in spite of that, nevertheless, nonetheless, on the contrary, on the other hand, otherwise, still, yet

Emphasis

above all, certainly, especially, in any event, in fact, in other words, in particular, indeed, most important, surely

Exemplification

as an example, as an illustration, for example, for instance, in other words, in particular, specifically, that is

Place

above that, at this point, below that, beyond that, here, nearby, next to that, on the other side, outside, within

Reason

for this purpose, for this reason, to this end

Result

accordingly, as a consequence, as a result, consequently, for that reason, hence, inevitably, necessarily, that being the case, then, therefore, thus

Summary

as has been noted, as I have said, finally, in brief, in other words, in short, in sum, last, on the whole, to be sure, to sum up

Time

after a while, afterward, at last, at length, at once, before, briefly, by degrees, eventually, finally, first (second, third, etc.), gradually, immediately, in a short time, in the future, in the meantime, instantaneously, later, meanwhile, promptly, slowly, soon, suddenly

4.   In most paragraphs, mix your transitional devices: combine pronoun reference, repetition of important

words, and transitional expressions to achieve the most effective continuity:

The reason for the mixture is quite simple: repetition dulls, but variety sharpens, interest. Look at the next paragraph, for example, where the writer balances pronoun reference (*we, us, our*), repetition of important words (*teen-agers, teen-years, teens*), and transitional expressions (*for instance, on the other hand*)—to get continuity *and* interest.

Pronoun (referring back to teen-agers)

Pronoun

Transitional expression

Pronoun

Pronoun

And since we [teen-agers] are so new, many people have some very wrong ideas about us. For instance, the newspapers are always carrying advice-columns telling our mothers how to handle us, their "bewildered maladjusted offspring," and the movies portray us as half-witted bops; and in the current best sellers, authors recall their own confused, unhappy youth. On the other hand, speakers tell us that these teen-years are the happiest and freest of our lives, or hand us the "leaders of tomorrow, forge on the future" line. The general opinion is that teen-agers are either car-stealing, dope-taking delinquents, or immature, weepy adolescents with nothing on our minds

Transitional expression

Pronoun

Important word

Pronoun

Repetition of important word

but boys (or girls as the case may be). Most adults have one of two attitudes toward the handling of teens—some say that only a sound beating will keep us in line; others treat us as mentally unbalanced creatures on the brink of insanity, who must be pampered and shielded at any cost.

Repetition of important word

Pronoun

—Judith D. Matz, "The New Third Age"
(*American Judaism*, Winter 1964–65)

In brief, don't make your readers jump desperately from one idea to another, like a flea changing dogs; use your transitions to *carry* them across the gaps between sentences. *Get continuity in orderly arrangement; point out the continuity with transitional devices—pronoun reference, repetition of important words, and transitional expressions.*

tri

Trite Ideas—Do not permit yourself to express trite ideas as though they were fresh, novel, original observations.

Trite ideas are commonplaces—ideas expressed so frequently that they have lost interest and become stale and vapid. They are characterized by worn-out expressions, treatments, or points of view. They are platitudes decorated with clichés.

When your instructor marks an idea *trite*, then, he or she means that you have not thought for yourself in your own language. Such a passage can be revised only by rethinking and rewriting it in its entirety.

For instance, this trite idea cannot simply be rephrased: "In today's complex world a college education is necessary for success." *In today's complex world* is a cliché; the entire idea itself is, first, commonplace; second, obvious; and third, with a little *original* thinking, rather questionable. What is *success*, for example? Happiness? Security? Wealth? And why *necessary*? Do *all* successful people have college educations? What about Harry Truman, a "successful" politician? What about the Beatles, "successful" musicians?

In other words, trite ideas must be inserted into a mental microscope, scrutinized carefully, and then discarded, once you've recorded your *real* observations. Don't let the world do your thinking—or your writing—for you.

(See **Cliché.**)

u **Unity**—Achieve unity by making sure each sentence in your paragraph is directly related to the idea expressed by your topic sentence.

Unity means oneness—and you get it by sticking to your main idea, by making sure every sentence carries its part of the burden instead of drifting off into unrelated ideas.

Take for example the following paragraph. It has unity; it hangs together as a whole. Note that the first sentence states the main idea. As you read the paragraph, note how the writer illustrates his contention. Every sentence turns on this point, his main idea.

> For the homeless, Los Angeles is a favored city. One seldom needs a heated grate for sleeping, or the Army greatcoat, long-time skid-row fashion in colder climate. Somehow, with his tan and his great growth of hair—what is the explanation for the rarity of baldness among residents of skid row?—the derelict in Los Angeles appears to be a healthier specimen

than his brethren elsewhere. One is struck, too, by the number of women who work the trash baskets and doze in the musty hallways.

> —William S. Ellis, "Los Angeles:
> City in Search of Itself"
> (*National Geographic,* January 1979)

Stick to the main idea and you can't go wrong. This sounds simple enough. But look at how quickly you can stray off into unrelated ideas. Watch what happens as a student argues that we are becoming a nation of cheaters. His first two sentences set up the main idea and give an example to support it—but sentence three catches at *another* idea: the reasons for cheating. This is undoubtedly suggested by the main idea, but it does not carry out the main idea; instead, it drifts off into a little story about last night's "date," splitting the paragraph into two pieces. The sense of unity is lost; the feeling of oneness is broken.

(1) You don't have to look very far to see that just about everyone, in one way or another, cheats, apparently with the approval of their family and friends, which makes them cheaters too. *(2)* For example, my father pads his expense account every time he goes on a business trip. *(3)* Of course, one of the reasons Americans cheat is that everything is so

expensive. *(4)* Just last night I took out a girl who wanted an orchid corsage. *(5)* That was five dollars. *(6)* And then there was the price of the dinner (ten dollars), admission to the dance (four-fifty), and a snack afterwards (four dollars). *(7)* All together, she cost me twenty-three-fifty, but we had so much fun it was worth the money. *(8)* So, like everyone else I cheat too—because I have to.

In short, only sentences 1 and 2 stick to the point; sentences 3–8 skip off into other ideas, and the paragraph loses unity.

To achieve unity, then, you must make absolutely certain that each sentence in your paragraph is directly related to the idea expressed by your topic sentence.

(See **Topic Sentence.**)

---

usg   **Usage**—For most writing, choose words from the general vocabulary of Standard English: that is, use language appropriate to your subject and your audience.

Standard English is the spoken and written language of educated men and women. Nonstandard English is the language of illiterate people, of certain dialect groups, and of some minorities.

Standard English

Standard English, the linguists tell us, consists of three varieties which shade into one another: Informal English, General English, and Formal English.

1.   Informal English

Informal English, more often spoken than written, is the language used by educated people in private conversations, personal letters, and that writing—such as some fiction—intended to be close to popular speech. Informal English is characterized by colloquial words and constructions (such expressions as *goings on, hasn't got, exam,* and *no go,* and contractions like *don't, it's,* and *we'd*) and by slang. Slang is, as Stuart Berg Flexner writes in his *Dictionary of American Slang,* "the body of words and expressions frequently used by or intelligible to a rather large portion of the general American public, but not accepted as good, formal usage by the majority." Slang includes words and expressions such as *goof off, humungous, phony, screwed-up, flip off, son-of-a-bitch, scram, make a scene, jump the gun, enthuse, bum, creep,* and *big shot.* Most college desk dictionaries employ usage labels for colloquialisms and slang.

In addition to the special flavor of its vocabulary, Informal English tends to use a less tightly organized sentence structure—a loose structure consisting largely of main clauses standing alone as complete sentences, or joined by coordinating conjunctions to form compound sentences. Just as often, however, Informal English relies on run-together sentences, sentence fragments, and partially completed phrases, supplemented by gestures, facial expressions, and intonation to make meanings clear. Thus the written language, when it attempts to reproduce colloquial English accurately, in actuality simplifies the spoken language by reducing this mélange to printed symbols.

Although some instructors find it acceptable, *as a rule Informal English is not appropriate to college writing.* Hence most errors in usage will require that you change the offending word or construction from Informal (or sometimes Nonstandard) English to General English.

2.   General English

General English, both spoken and written, is appropriate to almost any subject or any audience. Its tone may range from the extremely formal to the very informal, but its vocabulary consists largely of those words—*not* labeled by dictionaries—used by educated men and women. Thus General English, in practice, is a literary language, used in business letters, advertising copy, book reviews, written examinations, student essays, professional fiction and nonfiction of all sorts, and an extensive variety of other writing. The constructions employed in General English are those considered "correct" by educated people.

3. Formal English

Formal English, almost exclusively a written language, is characterized by a precise, extensive vocabulary, with a high proportion of words derived from Latin and Greek. It uses a tighter, more complex structure than either of the other two varieties of Standard English. Formal English is appropriate to formal occasions—technical and scientific reports, academic writing, books and articles written for professional groups. It is appropriate to *some* college writing, but it often sounds wooden and stilted, and for that reason perhaps ought to be left to the academics who are coerced by convention into using it, or to the scoundrels who, having nothing to say, take refuge in it.

Nonstandard English

Nonstandard English is the speech of uneducated men and women. It is characterized by socially unacceptable —and therefore "ungrammatical"—constructions such as the double negative ("He don't have none") and by words such as *ain't*. In addition, it uses many words and constructions confined to limited regions. Hence the speech of the ignorant white Southerner differs radically from that of the Pennsylvania Dutch farm boy or the Seattle ghetto child—but all three may speak forms of Nonstandard English.

We want to make it indisputably clear, however, that we do not condemn Nonstandard English as bad English. Both authors of this book grew up speaking varieties of Nonstandard English, one of us as a small-town Texas boy, the other as a street-child in a Chicago ghetto. But as it is the business of colleges and universities to educate men and women, it is also their business to give their graduates a language in which ideas can be discussed with dignity and sophistication. So you must not think that your instructors are assaulting your rightful linguistic heritage—or attacking you personally—when they criticize a usage that comes naturally to you but does not belong to Standard English. They are simply doing their job, a necessary one if you come to college with the best of motives—to acquire an education.

(See **Glossary of Usage.**)

Wordiness—Cut out every unnecessary word.

Gustave Flaubert once advised, "Whenever you can shorten a sentence, do. And one always can. The best sentence? The shortest." Pliny the Younger, we are told, ended a letter by saying, "I apologize for this long letter; I didn't have time to shorten it." Dr. Johnson urged us, "Read over your compositions, and when you meet with a passage which you think is particularly fine, strike it out."

The worst sentences, then, are puffed up with mere words, stuffed with the soft bombast of insubstantial, cottony diction. To write well, cut out the padding. Leave the hard, rigid frame of each sentence.

ORIGINAL	REVISION
Good and effective writing is not done in accordance with a set of rules with which we guide	Good writing is produced not by rules but by taste, intelligence, and sensitivity.

ORIGINAL

REVISION

ourselves, but with taste, intelligence, and sensitivity, which are among the best guides of all. (Be wary of long, empty phrases like *in accordance with.* Watch your *which*-clauses.)

In the fast-moving world of today in which we are faced with many important and significant global problems, not the least of which is the critical effect of the energy crisis on the world in which we live. (*In the fast-moving world of today* is a crutch on which millions of students have hobbled through empty sentences. *In which we live* seems rather obvious—and why repeat it, except in desperation? The *critical* effect of the energy *crisis*? Certainly the word *critical* is unnecessary. Avoid passive constructions like *we are faced.*)

Today we face many important problems; the most important is perhaps the energy crisis.

(See **Awkward Phrasing** and **Sentence Structure/Style.**)

Wrong Word—Use each word in its proper sense or senses.

WW

A word marked *Wrong Word* simply doesn't belong: it exists, certainly, but it does not fit into the sentence you have forced it into, as you will see by studying the meanings of the word in any good dictionary. Using the wrong word not only confuses your reader: it obscures your meaning, and it marks your paper with the stamp of ignorance.

Never write without frequently consulting a good dictionary.

ORIGINAL

Eloise was rushed to the *infirmity* after she fell down the laundry chute. (*Infirmity* means "defect or illness," not a place.)

She had a *pendant* for saying the wrong thing at the wrong time. (*Pendant* does not mean "a strong leaning." It means "a hanging ornament.")

REVISION

Eloise was rushed to the *infirmary* after she fell down the laundry chute. (*Infirmary* means "a place where injured or sick people are medically treated." We assume that is what this student meant.)

She had a *penchant* for saying the wrong thing at the wrong time.

Man is not a *pragmatic* animal; he
is *precarious*. (When *two* words
are obviously misused, one can
only guess at the writer's
meaning.)

(See **Awkward Phrasing.**)

Every book ought to have a conclusion. Let us once
again end our little book with a pregnant, enigmatic
observation by one of the ancient wise: "Out of nothing,
nothing can come, and nothing can become nothing"
(Persius). Good writing!

The Research Paper

Put in the simplest terms, the research paper is a writing assignment, usually requiring research in the library. We say "usually" because materials for such papers may also be acquired from experiments, interviews, speeches, films, and so on. Typically, the research paper is longer than other papers you are asked to write throughout a course. It represents an in-depth treatment of a particular subject, either assigned by the instructor or chosen by you.

Too often students regard the assignment of a research paper as a diabolical plot on the part of their instructors. Such an assignment need not be boring or frightening, however; it can, in fact, be a profitable and enjoyable experience. The research paper can help you with the kind of writing that will be required of you in courses other than English and give you practice in research, organization, and writing methods that will be valuable long after you leave school. As you proceed with your paper, it is quite possible that you will actually enjoy acquiring a degree of expertise in your subject and discovering new insights and relationships.

Choosing the Topic

Unless your instructor assigns a particular subject for your research paper, your first step is to choose a topic. Everyone is interested in something. What interests you? If you are a film buff, you might investigate William Randolph Hearst's reaction to the classic *Citizen Kane*. What do you want to know more about? If you are considering a career in medical technology, you might check on fields of specialization, skill requirements, and so on. Select a topic that you are interested in learning more about. Discuss your choice with your instructor. He or she can probably tell you whether the topic is practical in terms of the kind and amount of information available.

Narrowing the Topic

After you have chosen or been assigned a general topic, you will probably need to narrow the subject and to decide strategy—whether the paper is to be argumentative or informational. One good place to start is by looking at general reference works such as encyclopedias— Americana or Britannica for example—under appropriate headings to get a general view of your topic. This may help you decide what facet of the subject you wish to investigate and what your strategy will be. In the case of some topics, your own experience and observations may give you a start.

Suppose, for example, you choose running as a topic. Quickly you discover that running can cause injuries. And so you have a tentative thesis statement:

> Running is hazardous to your body because it can cause various kinds of injuries.

As your blueprint, such a thesis statement tells you that after your introduction, your paper requires that you link running with various kinds of injuries.

Or perhaps you might want to give an explanation of what kinds of injuries are caused by running. Thus your tentative thesis statement—in this case an informational one—might look like this:

> Running can cause "runner's knee" and lower-leg, ankle, and foot injuries.

Again, the thesis statement provides you with a blueprint for organizing your paper: first an introduction, next a section dealing with how running can injure the knee, then a section dealing with how it can injure the lower leg, and so on. In any case the thesis statements above are not fixed or unchangeable: they are tentative. Treat your thesis as a hypothesis, subject to reshaping in the light of new evidence.

The Detective Work

Now find material. First, try the card catalogue in your library. The card catalogue lists each book in the library at least three times: by author's name, last name first; by title of the book; by subject or topic. Your best bet is to look under your topic. Each card usually contains enough information to indicate whether or not the book will be of any use. If it is, list it and all other books you find by call number, author, title, and publication data (publisher, place of publication, and copyright date) on a piece of paper or, better yet, on 4″ × 6″ cards. Take good care of these cards: later much of what is on them will become your bibliography.

For two reasons, it is a good idea not to go to the stacks for your books until you feel your list is complete. First, you'll need to make only one trip. Second, expect at least half the books you want to be checked out of the library. Thus, if some books aren't available, you can simply continue down the shelves in search of the next one on your list *ad nauseam*.

But your list isn't complete until you look at the periodicals. Periodicals are more current. (It usually takes as long to publish a book as it does to have a baby—about nine months.) To find appropriate periodicals, consult the *Reader's Guide to Periodical Literature*, which is published twice each month except during July and August. *Reader's Guide* is alphabetically arranged by author's last name and topic. Once again, your best bet is to search out your topic and the appropriate subheading.

Another index worth looking at is the *New York Times Index*, published twice each month. Over the years, the *New York Times* has been an important resource for most scholars: it is regarded by many as the most reliable day-by-day chronicle of the United States.

There are other indexes, such as the pamphlet file, in which to find leads to useful material. But for these indexes, ask the help of your reference librarians, who always seem to know what is where and how to put one's hands on it. Most reference librarians are eager to help you.

Finally, before proceeding to the next stage—gathering information from these books, magazines, etc.—ask yourself what might be available in the community. For example, for a paper on abortion, especially one in favor of it, The Planned Parenthood Association, with offices in most communities, is a gold mine of information. If your subject is related to governmental activities, especially on the local level, the local League of Women Voters is a rich source of material. You might get some vital information or references by interviewing local politicians or board members. If the subject is related to the hazards of cigarette smoking or pollution, try the local offices of the American Cancer Society or the American Lung Association. Chances are the publications of these two organizations will either give you the data you need or else indicate where it can be found. Here, again, interviews—if you can get them—with qualified medical personnel such as lung surgeons or heart specialists no doubt will prove useful. In certain situations, the *best* source—perhaps the only source—may be the interview. Such a situation could develop if, for example, you opted to argue in favor of capital punishment. There are few pieces of writing from that side of the issue to match the arguments of opponents such as Michael V. Di Salle or Thorsten Sellin. Under the circumstances, interviews with an assistant district attorney, for example, might turn up useful material. One caution, however: it's not good practice to waste an interviewee's time. Therefore, arrive equipped with knowledgeable questions written out, but be flexible enough to follow up answers that suggest further questions, questions not on your list. Do your best to get accurate notes. With the permission of the interviewee, use a tape recorder.

Note Taking

Use either 3″ × 5″ or 4″ × 6″ cards for notes—*one note per book, magazine article, etc., per card* no matter whether that note be a paraphrase or a direct quotation. Why only one note per card? For reasons of organizational flexibility. You will be shuffling these cards to adjust any organizational changes you make. Two notes on one card present a problem: what do you do if one note belongs in one place in the organizational plan and the second note in another? Second, make certain that each card identifies the source of the material including page number(s). Hint: instead of writing title and author on each card, assign all entries in your bibliography a number and simply use these numbers on your cards for identification.

As you take notes, always be sure to use quotation marks around directly quoted material. To avoid the possibility of plagiarism it is a good idea to take information verbatim from your sources. In this way you will be able to keep track of when and how you are rephrasing versus directly quoting information in your final paper, without going back to each source.

When you have finished taking notes, organize your cards into cohesive groups according to the various points covered. For example, if your topic is the kinds of injuries that can be caused by running, one stack of cards will deal with introductory material on what these injuries are. Another stack will include a definition, description, etc., of "runner's knee"; the next stack with lower-leg injuries; the next with ankle injuries; and the next with foot injuries. If your teacher requires that you submit an outline for your paper, don't panic. By sorting and grouping the note cards, you are creating the basis for an outline.

Footnotes

Footnote all direct quotations. Failure to enclose such material in quotation marks and to acknowledge the source leaves you open to charges of plagiarism.

Some hints about direct quotations:

1. Always provide a lead-in for all direct quotations:

   H. L. Mencken reports that for twenty-six years Edgar Allan Poe's grave was unmarked because "The stonecutter . . . was preparing to haul it [a plain stone] to the churchyard when a runaway freight-train smashed into his stoneyard and broke the stone to bits. Thereafter the Poes seem to have forgotten Cousin Edgar: at all events nothing further was done."[1]

2. Directly quote those opinions or factual details that you want to stand out; paraphrase—put in your own words—everything else so that your paper sounds like you.

3. Use ellipsis points—three periods (. . .) a type space apart—in place of words or whole sentences omitted from

---

[1] H. L. Mencken, "Three American Immortals," *Prejudices: A Selection*, ed. James T. Farrell (New York: Vintage Books, 1954), p. 44.

a direct quotation either for lack of importance or pertinence as in the first sentence in the example under hint number one.

4.   Use brackets to interrupt a direct quotation for an editorial comment. For example, should you come across an error in the material being quoted, insert [sic]—"thus it is in the original"—immediately following the error:

> The Livermore News reported that "Mrs. Berry is a highly taunted [sic] member of Naive [sic] Daughters of the Golden West."

Also use brackets to make an editorial insertion at a given point in the quotation as an aid to clarity. Brackets were used for that purpose in the first sentence of the example under hint number one.

5.   For direct quotations of approximately fifty words or more, single space, indent margins left and right, and do not use quotation marks.

> Where, then, did Poe's tombstone come from? Mencken explains it this way:

> The existing tombstone was erected by a committee of Baltimore schoolmarms and cost about $1,000. It took the dear girls ten long years to raise the money. They started out with a "literary entertainment" which yielded $380. This was in 1865. Six years

later the fund had made such slow progress that, with accumulated interest, it came to but $587.02. Three years more went by: it now reached $627.66. Then some anonymous Poeista came down with $100, two others gave $50 each, one of the devoted schoolmarms raised $52 in nickels and dimes, and George W. Childs agreed to pay any remaining deficit. During all this time not a single American author of position gave the project any aid.[2]

Footnote paraphrased material outside the realm of common knowledge. For example, it is common knowledge that Walt Whitman wrote *Leaves of Grass*. But the fact that he was fired in 1865 from his $600-a-year clerk's job in the U.S. Department of the Interior for being a poet is not. Therefore such material should be footnoted. *If in doubt, footnote.*

FORMAT FOR FOOTNOTING

The research paper is based on information or opinions gathered from several sources, and footnotes are your means of giving credit to those sources. While there are many systems of footnoting, the most widely accepted is that established by the Modern Language Association in its *MLA Handbook*.

[2] Mencken, p. 45

Numbering

Footnotes are numbered consecutively with Arabic numbers, starting with number 1. These numbers correspond with the numbers assigned to the materials in the text requiring documentation. In the body of the paper the number is placed one-half space above the line and after the material to be footnoted. In the footnote itself, the number precedes the acknowledgment, is indented five spaces, and is placed one-half space above the line.

Placement

Footnotes go at the bottom of the page containing the material to be acknowledged or on a separate page at the end of the paper and before the bibliography. When footnotes are placed at the bottom of the page, they are sometimes separated from the body of the paper by a short line starting at the left-hand margin. Most of the time, however, footnotes begin two spaces below the last line of copy. When footnotes appear at the bottom of the page, they are single spaced, with the first line indented five spaces; double spacing is used between footnotes. When they appear at the end of the paper, they are usually double spaced.

Primary footnotes, those given the first time a source is mentioned, generally contain four components: name of author, title of work, data regarding publication, and page number(s).

Footnote for a book:

> Jacques P. Thiroux, *Ethics: Theory and Practice*, 2nd ed. (Encino, Ca.: Glencoe, 1980), p. 300.

Footnote for a magazine article:

> Carol Bly, "The Last of the Gold Star Mothers," *The New Yorker*, September 24, 1979, p. 36.

If the volume number is given, then the symbol "p." or "pp." for page or pages is dropped:

> John Rouse, "The Politics of Composition," *College English*, 41, No. 1 (September 1979), 1–12.

(Further primary footnotes appear in the section comparing footnote and bibliographical forms.)

Secondary footnotes: After you have used a primary footnote, refer to the same source with a shortened form, usually just the name of the author and page:

> Thiroux, p. 300.

If more than one work by the same author is being used, include the title of the work:

> Bly, "The Last of the Gold Star Mothers," p. 36.

Ibid., an abbreviation of the Latin *ibidem*, "in the same place," is sometimes used to refer to the footnote immediately preceding, *provided both footnotes are on the same page*; otherwise the shortened form (author and page) is used. Thus *Ibid.* means previous source, same page. *Ibid.* plus *p.* means same source but a different page.

Jacques P. Thiroux, *Ethics: Theory and Practice,* 2nd ed. (Encino, Ca.: Glencoe, 1980), p. 300.

Ibid. (or)

Thiroux, p. 300.

If the page number is different:

Ibid., p. 301. (or)

Thiroux, p. 301.

Op. cit. and *loc. cit.,* once employed extensively in secondary footnotes, are unnecessarily confusing and no longer used.

Bibliography

The bibliography is a list of all sources used in the research paper. This includes not only published works, such as books and articles, but interviews and experiments. The bibliography appears as the last item in the research paper. Entries are alphabetized by author's last name. Unlike footnotes, bibliography citations are not indented but begin at the left-hand margin. All subsequent lines are indented five spaces. Entries may be single spaced with double spacing between them or double spaced throughout. Differences and similarities between bibliography and footnote citations are shown in the following section.

Bibliography and Footnote Forms

BOOKS

One author

Bibliography

Poole, Shona Crawford. *The Christmas Cookbook*. New York: Atheneum, 1979.

Footnote

¹Shona Crawford Poole, *The Christmas Cookbook* (New York: Atheneum, 1979), p. 14.

Two authors

Bibliography

Horowitz, I. A., and Fred Reinfeld. *How to Think Ahead in Chess*. New York: Simon & Schuster, 1964.

Footnote

²I. A. Horowitz and Fred Reinfeld, *How to Think Ahead in Chess* (New York: Simon & Schuster, 1964), p. 43.

More than three authors

Bibliography

Van Nostrand, A. D., et al. *Functional Writing*. Boston: Houghton Mifflin, 1978.

Footnote

[3] A. D. Van Nostrand et al., *Functional Writing* (Boston: Houghton Mifflin, 1978), p. 8.

Anonymous author

Bibliography

H.E.L.P.: *Home Energy Ladies' Pal* (Canoga Park, Ca.: Xyzyx Information Corp., 1972), p. 42.

Footnote

[4] *H.E.L.P.: Home Energy Ladies' Pal* (Canoga Park, Ca.: Xyzyx Information Corp., 1972), p. 42.

Organizational authorship

Bibliography

Exploring Energy Choices. Washington, D.C.: The Ford Foundation, 1974.

Footnote

[5] *Exploring Energy Choices* (Washington, D.C.: The Ford Foundation, 1974), p. 3.

New edition

Bibliography

Houp, Kenneth W., and Thomas E. Pearsall. *Reporting Technical Information*, 4th ed. Encino, Ca.: Glencoe, 1980.

Footnote

[6] Kenneth W. Houp and Thomas E. Pearsall, *Reporting Technical Information*, 4th ed. (Encino, Ca.: Glencoe, 1980), p. 24.

Editor(s)

Bibliography

Adelstein, Michael E., and Jean G. Pival, eds. *Women's Liberation*. New
    York: St. Martin's Press, 1972.

Footnote

   [7] Michael E. Adelstein and Jean G. Pival, eds., *Women's Liberation*
(New York: St. Martin's Press, 1972), pp. 35–36.

More than one volume

Bibliography

Gottesman, Ronald, et al., eds. *The Norton Anthology of American
    Literature*. 2 vols. New York: Norton, 1979.

Footnote

   [8] Ronald Gottesman et al., eds., *The Norton Anthology of American
Literature* (New York: Norton, 1979), II, 180.

(Note: After volume number, page symbol—*p.* or *pp.*—is
dropped.)

Translation

Bibliography

Serullaz, Maurice. *French Painting: The Impressionist Painters*. Trans.
    W. J. Strachan. New York: Universe Books, n.d.

Footnote

   [9] Maurice Serullaz, *French Painting: The Impressionist Painters*,
trans. W. J. Strachan (New York: Universe Books, n.d.), pp. 33–35.

(**Note:** n.d. means no date is included in your source. When no publisher or place of publication is included, use n.p. When pages are not numbered, indicate n.pag.—no pagination—in place of page numbers.)

Part of a series

Bibliography

Kennard, Jean E. *The Literature of the Absurd*. Harper Studies in
Language and Literature. New York: Harper & Row, 1975.

Footnote

[10]Jean E. Kennard, *The Literature of the Absurd*, Harper Studies in
Language and Literature (New York: Harper & Row, 1975), p. 12.

Series with editor

Bibliography

Shakespeare, William. *Twelfth Night*. Ed. T. H. Howard-Hill. Blackfriars
Shakespeare. Dubuque: Wm. C. Brown, 1969.

Footnote

[11]William Shakespeare, *Twelfth Night*, ed. T. H. Howard-Hill,
Blackfriars Shakespeare (Dubuque: Wm. C. Brown, 1969), p. 24.

Introduction

Bibliography

Collins, Wilkie. *The Moonstone*. New York: The Heritage Press, 1959.

Footnote

[12] Vincent Starrett, "Introduction," *The Moonstone*, by Wilkie Collins (New York: The Heritage Press, 1959), pp. xiii–xiv.

(**Note:** In the bibliography, the book is referred to in its totality. Hence it is referred to by its author. In the footnote, the specific component of the book is referred to.)

Editor's foreword (preface or introduction) to an anthology

Bibliography

Hardy, John Edward, ed. "Foreword." *The Modern Talent.* New York: Holt, Rinehart & Winston, 1964.

Footnote

[13] John Edward Hardy, ed., "Foreword," *The Modern Talent* (New York: Holt, Rinehart & Winston, 1964), p. vi.

Classics: Plays

Bibliography

Hamlet.

Footnote

[14] *Hamlet* IV.vii.70–75.

(**Note:** Capital Roman numerals are acts; lower case Roman numerals, scenes; Arabic numerals, lines. Note that commas are not used after titles, and periods—not commas—separate main divisions.)

Classics: Poetry

Bibliography
Milton *Paradise Lost.*

Footnote
        [15] Milton *Paradise Lost* V. 117–208.

(**Note:** Capital Roman numerals stand for books, Arabic numerals for lines. Note punctuation.)

The Bible

Bibliography
The Bible.

(**Note:** The Bible is never italicized.)

Footnote
        [16] Psalms 12:3–6.

(**Note:** Parts of the Bible are never italicized; in this example, "12" is the chapter, and "3–6" are verses.)

ENCYCLOPEDIA ARTICLES

Signed article, general encyclopedia, alphabetically arranged

Bibliography
Brodie, Bernard. "Command of the Pacific." *Encyclopaedia Britannica,* 1960.

Footnote
    [17] Bernard Brodie, "Command of the Pacific," *Encyclopaedia Britannica,* 1960.

(**Note:** No volume and page numbers are required when the reference work is alphabetically arranged. No place of publication and publisher are needed for any general encyclopedia.)

Unsigned article, general encyclopedia, alphabetically arranged

Bibliography
"Pacific Grove." *Encyclopaedia Britannica,* 1960.

Footnote
    [18] "Pacific Grove," *Encyclopaedia Britannica,* 1960.

Signed article, specialized encyclopedia, alphabetically arranged

Bibliography

Acton, H. B. "The Absolute." *Encyclopedia of Philosophy*. New York: Macmillan, 1967.

Footnote

[19] H. B. Acton, "The Absolute," *Encyclopedia of Philosophy* (New York: Macmillan, 1967).

MAGAZINES, NEWSPAPERS

Signed article

Bibliography

Revzin, Philip. "Gold-Price Rise Warns of Big Dangers Ahead." *The Wall Street Journal*, September 28, 1979, p. 1, col. 6; p. 27, cols. 1–4.

Footnote

[20] Philip Revzin, "Gold-Price Rise Warns of Big Dangers Ahead," *The Wall Street Journal*, September 28, 1979, p. 27, col. 3.

(Note: Bibliography cites entire article. Footnote gives only that portion actually used in research paper.)

Bibliography

Lees, Elaine O. "Evaluating Student Writing." *College Composition and Communication*, XXX, No. 4 (December 1979), 370–74.

Footnote

[21] Elaine O. Lees, "Evaluating Student Writing," *College Composition and Communication*, XXX, No. 4 (December 1979), 373.

(**Note:** Volume numbers are frequently applied to scholarly journals that appear monthly, quarterly, or annually. In the above citation, "XXX" is the volume number and "No. 4" is the issue number of that volume. Page designation—p. or pp.—is dropped when volume number is used.)

Unsigned article

Bibliography

"The Mystery of Sudden Infant Death." *Consumer Reports*, June 1975, pp. 363–65.

Footnote

[22] "The Mystery of Sudden Infant Death," *Consumer Reports*, June 1975, p. 363.

Editorial

Bibliography

Editorial. San Francisco *Chronicle*, 29 May 1975, Sec.3, p.36, cols.1–2.

Footnote

[23] Editorial, San Francisco *Chronicle*, 29 May 1975, Sec.3, p.36, cols.1–2.

MISCELLANEOUS

Pamphlet with author

Bibliography

Fredrickson, Donald T. *How to Stop Smoking!* New York: American
Heart Association, 1969.

Footnote

[24] Donald T. Fredrickson, *How to Stop Smoking!* (New York:
American Heart Association, 1969), p. 2.

Pamphlet without author

Bibliography

The Heart and Blood Vessels. New York: American Heart Association,
1973.

Footnote

[25] *The Heart and Blood Vessels* (New York: American Heart
Association, 1973), pp. 13–15.

Interview

Bibliography

Interview with three convicted plagiarists. San Mateo County Jail.
Redwood City, Ca., June 20, 1976.

Footnote

[26] Interview with three convicted plagiarists, San Mateo County Jail,
Redwood City, Ca., June 20, 1976.

Speech

Bibliography

Platt, Bradley K. "Colombian Cuisine." Ames, November 21, 1976.
    (Speech delivered at Iowa State University Student Union.)

Footnote

    [27] Bradley K. Platt, "Colombian Cuisine," Speech delivered at Iowa
State University Student Union, Ames, November 21, 1976.

Sample Research Paper

THE DUAL PURPOSE OF OUR NATIONAL PARKS

Cathy L. Stephenson

English 103
Dr. Silliman
March 12, 1980

OUTLINE

THESIS: Continuation of the dual purpose of our
          national parks--preservation and use--
          requires that the National Park Service
          policy be revised.

   I. Dual purpose

      A. Future preservation
         1. Nature preserves
         2. Natural forces
            a. Fire
            b. Water
      B. Public use

  II. Present conditions

      A. Vehicles
         1. Atmosphere
         2. Ranger's time
         3. Visitor safety
      B. Visitor capacity
      C. Commercialization
         1. Visitor's needs
         2. Commercial establishments

III. Proposals for the future
    A. Closure to cars
    B. Visitor arrangements
       1. Specialized areas
       2. Private campgrounds
       3. Trails
          a. Bicycling
          b. Walking
          c. Horseback riding
       4. Tram service
    C. Limited commercial establishments

THE DUAL PURPOSE OF OUR NATIONAL PARKS

The long views, deep forests, clear
streams; the eagle, the mountain lion,
the antelope; solitude, tranquility for
men; a glimpse of eternity: these were
to be saved . . . before the march of
cities destroyed them everywhere.
    And so it was that Stephen Tyng
Mather, founder of the National Park
Service in 1916, established the
National Park Association on May 20,
1919.[1]

In this paper, the writer will discuss the
purpose of our national parks, the present
condition of the parks, and future proposals to
insure that this generation and those that follow
have equal opportunity to enjoy the benefits of
the parks. Special focus will be placed on
Yosemite National Park in Northern California
because of the publicity this fragile environment
has received during the past several years.
    The National Park Service Act of 1916 states
that the first purpose of our national parks is
the preservation of scenery and the maintenance of
natural and historic items of value and wildlife,

and that the second purpose is the enjoyment of the parks by visitors. The parks were initially established for the sustentation of these values, which must be compatible.[2]

The National Park Centennial Commission has recommended that nature preserves be set up in each park with an example of an ecosystem indigenous to each area.[3] For example, in Sequoia National Park, such a preserve would include sequoia trees, the High Sierra meadow, and other items native to this park. This recommendation may or may not be reasonable. Because the national parks themselves were set aside for this purpose and because the nature preserves would be set up so that visitors could see the ecosystem of the park, nature preserves would seem unnecessary.

However, one of the problems that has arisen in the parks is the restraint of natural forces such as fire and water. This has left each park with a changed environment.[4] And the change may be irrevocable. For example, the sequoia trees indigenous to Sequoia National Park are not reproducing because naturally caused fires, which would ordinarily burn out undergrowth and other trees such as lodgepole pine and white fir that compete with the sequoia tree for space, have been extinguished. A program of controlled burns is underway now in the park; this will clear out the undergrowth and pave the way for reforestation.

After this, every fire caused by natural forces, such as lightning, will be allowed to burn itself out. This should result in reforestation of the giant tree. Another example comes from the Grand Canyon in Arizona, where Hoover Dam on the Colorado River has caused many problems. The dam has altered the flow of the river so that it is no longer scouring the sides as it used to. In addition, the volume of the river has been halved, causing retention of sediment, which in turn causes severe rapids.[5] These man-made restraints of natural forces cause changes in the environments of our national parks and leave them impaired for future generations. For this reason, there indeed may be a need for preserves in which nature is allowed to take its course, leaving an example of the indigenous ecosystem for future generations to learn from and enjoy.

The second purpose of our national parks is the use and enjoyment of them by visitors. This purpose must be compatible with the first; otherwise there will be nothing left for future generations to enjoy. Visitor capacity and use of the parks have risen steadily since their creation, resulting in a strain on each park's fragile environment. Therefore, the National Park Service's present policy needs to be revised.

The present condition of our national parks has been under scrutiny lately by many people.

Environmental groups have been instrumental in pointing out the necessity for a public policy change. Among the areas that need to be investigated are use of vehicles, visitor capacity, and commercialization.

Vehicles in the parks are creating major problems such as air pollution, including view-obstructing smog.[6] Visitor safety is also a concern because of increasing traffic. Presently, rangers must spend time insuring visitor safety rather than concentrating on visitor education and enjoyment.[7]

The number of visitors to the parks has increased tremendously in the past few years. Between 1970 and 1977 there was an increase of 52,807 people in Yosemite National Park alone.[8] This increase of visitors has placed a strict demand on the facilities at the park. Campsite reservations have been initiated to help control the flood of campers to the park, and a limit of one week placed on their length of stay in order to keep the visitors flowing.[9] The increase in our population has placed large demands upon the parks. The people born in the baby boom of the early 1960s are now about twenty years old and represent a large portion of visitors to the parks. The growth of communities surrounding the parks has amplified day use of the parks, as has increased job pressure.[10]

Commercialization, too, has contributed to the necessity for a public park policy change. Our national parks should only service visitors' needs. They should not provide luxury items. The following paragraph appears in National Parks and Conservation Magazine:

> It [Yosemite] has world-acclaimed High Sierra scenery, traffic jams that are almost as famous, and a spanky new shuttle bus system that signals a pilot effort to declare war on congestion in the parks. It has "cathedral" forests of ancient sequoias; it has dramatic waterfalls, alpine meadows, and tacky stores— not to mention both pitch-and-putt and standard golf course, gas stations, barber shops, beauty shops, and bars.[11]

Visitors' needs in the national park include a place to stay, either a campsite or cabin-type housing, a place to buy groceries, and very little else. In the words of G. Frank Brockman,

> In planning for recreational use of the parks . . . the development should be related to their [the people's] inherent values and calculated to promote the beneficial use thereof by the people. It should not encourage exotic forms of amusement and should never permit that which conflicts with or weakens the enjoyment of these inherent values.[12]

Brockman also feels that

Roads, buildings, and other structures
necessary for park administration and for
public use and comfort should intrude upon the
landscape or conflict with it to the absolute
minimum.[13]

The National Park Centennial Commission
recommended that when new facilities are
considered for the needs of the visitors,
development outside of the park's boundaries be
looked at and "that the basic needs of the visitor
not be sacrificed. . . ."[14]

Another recommendation is to remove all so-
called luxury or unessential items. For Yosemite
this includes the barber and beauty shops, pools,
bank, car rental, sportswear shops, tennis courts,
ice rinks, the pitch-and-putt, and golf courses.
Housing for employees is to be removed to the
outer edges of the park, along with administrative
and maintenance offices.[15]

Obviously, the parks cannot continue to
accommodate increased visitors, commercialization,
and vehicles, and still maintain their dual
purpose. Something must be done. Closing the parks
to cars, revising visitor use policy, and limiting
commercial establishments will help to preserve
the park for future generations.

If the parks are closed to cars, atmospheric
conditions will improve, park rangers will have
more time to promote visitor education and

enjoyment, and visitor safety will be less of a concern to park officials. In the Yosemite Park Plan, which should be fully implemented in about ten years, cars will be allowed into the park but only in certain areas where parking spaces will be set up and tram service will run to all major areas of the park closed to cars. The park will be considered full only when the parking lots are filled. This has happened once in Yosemite's history--on their busiest day on record, Memorial Day 1976.[16]

In the Yosemite Park Plan, day-use visitors will be required to leave their vehicles near the entrance of the park and ride buses to all areas. Private campgrounds outside the park's boundaries will be encouraged, so that many campers will become day-use visitors. For campgrounds inside the park, trails will be set up to all areas. These will be for bicycling, walking, and horseback riding.[17] The stables will remain in the park, and campgrounds will be reserved exclusively for riders. The National Park Service intends to push these plans with all visitors to the parks in order to implement policy changes. For handicapped visitors, or people who simply do not enjoy strenuous activities, a tram service will be initiated. Trams will run to all campgrounds and attractions in the park every thirty minutes, except during peak seasons when they will run every fifteen minutes.

The third phase in the plan is to limit all commercial establishments and move all housing, maintenance, administrative offices, and unessentials to different areas in the park. At Yosemite, for example, most employee housing will be moved to El Portal. Administrative and maintenance offices will move to Wawona. Although, normally, luxury concessions would be eliminated entirely, in Yosemite they will be moved to Wawona because this has been known as an historical resort.

Because of the present conditions in our national parks, their dual purpose is not being carried out; therefore, the National Park Service policy needs to be revised. Implementation of the plans presented in this paper for all parks will preserve them for future generations and enable them to maintain their dual purpose of preservation and public use.

FOOTNOTES

1. Anthony Wayne Smith, ''Sixty Years,'' <u>National Parks and Conservation Magazine</u>, January 1979, p. 1.

2. Anthony Wayne Smith, ''Spaciousness,'' <u>National Parks and Conservation Magazine</u>, October 1977, p. 1.

3. National Parks Centennial Commission, Edmund R. Thornton, Chairman, <u>Preserving a Heritage: Final Report to the President and the Congress of the National Parks Centennial Commission</u> (Washington, D.C.: Government Printing Office, n.d.).

4. U.S., Department of Interior, National Park Service, ''Natural Processes Will Prevail,'' <u>Update: Yosemite General Management Plan</u> (Denver: National Park Service, August 1978), pp. 115–16.

5. Roy Johnson et al., ''Man's Impact on the Colorado River in the Grand Canyon,'' <u>National Parks and Conservation Magazine</u>, March 1977, p. 13.

6. U.S., Department of Interior, National Park Service, <u>Draft Environmental Statement: General Management Plan—Yosemite National Park</u>, Howard H. Chapman, Director (Denver: National Park Service, August 1978), p. 127.

7. Ibid., pp. 115–16.

8. George B. Hartzog, Jr., ''Clearing the Roads—and the Air—in Yosemite Valley,'' <u>National Parks and Conservation Magazine</u>, August 1972, p. 15.

9. Hartzog, p. 15.

10. U.S., Department of Interior, <u>Draft Environmental Statement</u>, p. 116.

11. ''A Long and Winding Road Back to Nature,'' <u>National Parks and Conservation Magazine</u>, December 1978, p. 21.

12. G. Frank Brockman, <u>Recreational Use of Wild Lands</u> (New York: McGraw-Hill, 1959), p. 131.

13. Ibid., p. 132.

14. National Parks Centennial Commission, p. 89.

15. Robert A. Jones, ''Park Service Would Limit Cars, Business in Yosemite,'' <u>Los Angeles Times</u>, 22 September 1978, Sec. 1, p. 21.

16. Jones, p. 21.

17. Hartzog, pp. 15–16.

BIBLIOGRAPHY

Brockman, G. Frank. <u>Recreational Use of Wild Lands</u>. New York: McGraw-Hill, 1959.

Hartzog, George B., Jr. "Clearing the Roads--and the Air--in Yosemite Valley." <u>National Parks and Conservation Magazine</u>, August 1972, pp. 14-17.

Johnson, R. Roy et al. "Man's Impact on the Colorado River in the Grand Canyon." <u>National Parks and Conservation Magazine</u>, March 1977, pp. 13-16.

Jones, Robert A. "Park Service Would Limit Cars, Business in Yosemite." <u>Los Angeles Times</u>, 22 September 1978, Sec. 1, p. 21.

"A Long and Winding Road Back to Nature." <u>National Parks and Conservation Magazine</u>, December 1978, pp. 21-23, 25.

National Parks Centennial Commission. Edmund R. Thornton, Chairman. <u>Preserving a Heritage: Final Report to the President and the Congress of the National Parks Centennial Commission</u>. Washington, D.C.: Government Printing Office, n.d.

Smith, Anthony Wayne. "Sixty Years." <u>National</u>

Parks and Conservation Magazine, January
1979, pp. 1, 31.

Smith, Anthony Wayne. "Spaciousness." National
Parks and Conservation Magazine, October
1977, pp. 1, 31.

U.S. Department of Interior. National Park
Service. Draft Environmental Statement:
General Management Plan—Yosemite National
Park. Howard H. Chapman, Chairman. Denver:
National Park Service, August 1978.

U.S. Department of Interior. National Park
Service. "Natural Processes Will Prevail."
Update: Yosemite General Management Plan.
Denver: National Park Service, August 1978.

The Essay Examination

The essay examination requires you to write in much the same way as you would for any assigned theme or composition—with two important differences: first, all of the information you use must come from your head; and second, you are usually required to write your essay(s) in a relatively short period of time, most often in one to three hours. Adequate preparation is therefore essential.

Preparing for the Exam

Carefully review all of the materials available to you. (1) Go over all of the textbooks assigned for the course. Check major headings, be sure you know all key terms, and make certain you can answer all of the exercises and assignments in the texts. (2) Reread all of your class notes. If any are missing, get them from a classmate. (3) Look over all of the past tests given in the course. Can you answer all of the questions? If not, ask your instructor or a reliable student for help. Many schools now have learning or tutorial centers where you can get professional or paraprofessional help in preparing for exams. Don't hesitate to ask for help wherever it's available. (4) Did you receive handouts, supplementary reading lists, or any other aids from the instructor? If so, review these thoroughly.

Next, try to figure out what essay questions are most likely to be asked. To what topics did the instructor devote the most lecture time? What points did he or she emphasize most heavily? On what topics or aspects of a topic were you assigned the most reading? In trying to determine what questions will be asked it is often helpful to get together with other students to assess various suggestions not only of the questions but also of the kinds of responses that will be most appropriate.

Although the suggestion is obvious, you would be wise to get plenty of sleep before the examination. Because you will be writing under some pressure, being well rested can give you the extra edge you may need to think and write quickly and effectively.

Examining the Exam

When you get the exam, read through the whole thing carefully. Do you have a choice of questions to answer? If so, decide which you will *not* answer, and put that question out of your mind. Now, if there is more than one question left, decide how much time you can spend on each. If one will give you more points than another, plan to devote more time to the one that will give you more credit. In calculating your time, allow five or ten minutes to go over what you have written, checking for obvious errors or omissions that you can correct quickly. Finally, decide which question you can answer most easily and prepare to tackle that question first.

Preparing to Write the Essay

Reread the question to make sure you understand precisely what is required in your essay. Look for certain key directions. For example, if you are asked to *summarize* a process, prepare to list the main steps in that process and the results of those steps. Note other key directions:

> illustrate: provide relevant examples
>
> define: give the precise meaning
>
> compare and contrast: show similarities and differences
>
> analyze: examine the various parts and how they relate to the whole
>
> evaluate: make a judgment of validity or worth, based on evidence
>
> interpret: explain what the facts indicate or imply

On a piece of scrap paper, jot down a rough thesis statement for your essay. Often you can formulate this guiding statement by rephrasing the directions. For example, suppose you are given this assignment: "Summarize the main causes of prison riots and analyze each cause." Your thesis might read like this: "The lessons of Attica and the New Mexico State Penitentiary teach us that there are three main causes of prison riots: overcrowding, racial tensions, and lack of firm control by prison officials."

Next jot down the main points stated in your thesis or the main supports for your thesis. In the case of our example you would probably write, "1. Overcrowding 2. Racial tensions 3. Lack of control by authorities." Then list a couple of statistics, examples, or details under each main point or support. Because your time is limited, allow one paragraph for your discussion of each main point.

Writing the Essay

If you have observed all the preliminaries, the actual writing of the essay will move swiftly, perhaps even painlessly. In the introductory paragraph state your thesis and explain the plan of your answer. In succeeding paragraphs deal with the main points you previously jotted down—one point per paragraph. Finally, compose a concluding paragraph in which you drive home your main points by rephrasing your thesis.

But wait—you are not quite finished. Take a few minutes to reread your essay in order to correct any mistakes or insert any other necessary information. If time allows, read slowly, checking spelling, grammar, and punctuation as well as content. Make all corrections neatly.

Another essay to write? Well, you already know the routine. ...

FORMS FOR LETTERS

There are two general classes of letters: business (formal) and personal (informal). Each kind is governed by the general principles of courtesy and clearness. But each has different forms and conventions.

Business Letters

These are formal and impersonal. A good business letter is clear, courteous, and brief. It shows who is writing, to whom, where, and when. It observes contemporary conventions of language, style, and form.

Use 8½ × 11 inch unlined white paper for business letters. Type on one side of the page only. Number each page consecutively in the top right-hand corner.

The business letter typically consists of the following parts:

1. *Heading:* the writer's full address and date. Do not use abbreviations for words like *Street, Avenue, East,* and *First.* Spell out the name of the state in full or use the correct Postal Service abbreviation (see **Abbreviations**). Type the date directly beneath the last line of the address. Do not abbreviate the name of the month.

In the full-block format described here, the heading begins flush (aligned) with the left margin. If you are using a company letterhead, type only the date, flush with the left margin and two lines below the last line of printed copy.

375 High Street
San Carlos, CA 94070
March 21, 1980

2.   *Inside address:* the full name and address of the person you're writing to, including zip code. The inside address always begins at the left margin.

Mr. Lewis Martin
Customer Relations Manager
Parnassus Optical Co., Inc.
1454 Elm Street
Palo Alto, CA 94303

Do not use abbreviations for words like *Street, Avenue, East,* and *First.* Spell out the name of the state in full or use the correct Postal Service abbreviation.

3.   *Salutation:* words used as the opening of the letter—that is, the "greeting," such as "Dear Mr. Martin." Type the salutation three spaces below the inside address, flush with the left margin.

The salutation always contains the recipient's title (*Mr., Ms., Mrs., Miss, Dr.,* etc.) and last name, followed by a colon, unless you are on a first-name basis with the recipient. Then you would use his or her title and full

name on the inside address but use only the first name in
the salutation.

> Dear Dr. Prost:
> Dear Mrs. Mace:
> Dear Ms. Chapman:
> Dear Marie:
>   *(first-name basis)*
> Dear Professor Robinson:

As the last example above shows, some titles are not
abbreviated in the salutation. As a general rule, abbreviate
only the titles *Mr., Mrs., Ms., Messrs.,* and *Dr.* All other
titles, such as *Professor, Father,* and *President,* should be
written in full.

If you're writing to a business or organization instead of
to a specific person, you have several options: you may
begin with an appropriate general term such as *Gentlemen*
or *Dear People* (the latter not yet accepted usage), or you
may use an "attention line," as in the example below:

> Parnassus Optical Co., Inc.
> 1454 Elm Street
> Palo Alto, CA 94303
>
> Attention: Customer Relations Department

When you're not certain whether the recipient is a man
or a woman, you may use a title appropriate to the context
of the letter.

Dear Customer Engineer:
    (letter to office equipment repair person)
Dear Homeowner:
    (letter from real estate agent)
Dear Writer:
    (letter from correspondence school)

4. *Body:* the text of your letter, divided into paragraphs and typed single-spaced with no indentations. Double-space between paragraphs.

If your letter is very short, however, you may increase both margins to about an inch and a half and double-space throughout, indicating paragraphs by indenting five spaces from the left.

5. *Complimentary close:* a conventional "goodbye," usually a standard expression such as "Sincerely yours," "Sincerely," or "Yours truly," typed flush left and followed by a comma. *Only the first letter of the close is capitalized.* Four spaces below, type your full name, aligned at the left with the close. If appropriate, type your business title on the line just below your name. Sign your name in the space between the complimentary close and your typed name. Sign your full name unless you are on a first-name basis with the recipient, in which case it is acceptable to sign only your given name.

6. *Additional information:* notations often required in business letters. These **include** *AKB*/*gwt* or *AKB:gwt* to

indicate that your letter was dictated to and typed by a secretary (with your initials first, in unspaced capital letters, followed by your secretary's in unspaced lowercase letters); *Enclosure: Title of Enclosure* to indicate that the writer is sending material along with the letter; *cc: Jan Wilson* to indicate that a carbon copy or photocopy was sent. Type the first notation flush left with the margin, two spaces below the last line of the complimentary close.

Sincerely yours,

Edgar G. Wallace

Edgar J. Wallace

EWG:gwt
Enclosure: Sabbatical Leave Report
cc: John W. Thomas
    Certificated Personnel Officer

In the form described above—full-block style—nothing is indented: all lines begin at the left margin. The letter is single-spaced throughout except for

1. five spaces between the return address and the inside address;

2. two spaces between the inside address and the salutation;
3. two spaces between the salutation and the first paragraph;
4. two spaces between each paragraph in the body;
5. two spaces between the last paragraph and the complimentary close;
6. four spaces between the complimentary close and the writer's typed name;
7. two spaces between the name and additional information if any.

The following pages indicate the form of the business letter and its envelope.

MODEL FOR BUSINESS LETTERS

375 High Street
San Carlos, CA 94070
March 21, 1980

Mr. Lewis Martin
Customer Relations
Parnassus Optical Co., Inc.
1454 Elm Street
Palo Alto, CA 94303

Dear Mr. Martin:

I am writing to ask about the
microcassette recorder (serial number
134450) I returned for repair on December
27 of last year. As I explained then, both
the built-in microphone and the optional
MMK-7 Electro-Condensor microphone seemed
to be recording noises from the machine

itself. I wanted to know if circuit
analysis would reveal any defects, and if
not whether you could suggest recording
techniques that would eliminate the
noises.

Unfortunately, I have not heard from your
company since I received a post card in
early January acknowledging receipt of my
tape recorder. I'm beginning to wonder if
it's been lost--or if there's another
explanation for the delay.

I would appreciate anything you can do to
see that my tape recorder is returned or
replaced as soon as possible. I need it
urgently.

Sincerely yours,

Martha St. John

Martha St. John

MSJ:gwt
Enclosure: Original Repair Request

MODEL FOR ADDRESSING BUSINESS ENVELOPES

Martha St. John
375 High Street
San Carlos, CA 94070

                        Mr. Martin Lewis
                        Customer Relations
                        Parnassus Optical Co., Inc.
                        1454 Elm Street
                        Palo Alto, CA 94303

The standard business envelope—designated No. 10 but
often called simply "a large envelope"—measures 9½ ×
4⅛ inches.

Personal Letters

The format for the personal letter is flexible: it may be written on lined paper of almost any size, or on scented 4 × 6 inch pastel stationery embellished with violets. You may use ink of a color that relects your curious tastes. If you prefer, you may type on 8½ × 11 inch white paper—a practice not recommended by the etiquette books. In short, depending on the degree of familiarity with the person you're writing to, almost anything goes, though the personal letter—like the business letter—should be courteous, clear, and neat.

As a general rule, the personal letter has the following parts:

1. your return address and date in the top right-hand corner;
2. the salutation—beginning at the left margin—about half an inch below the return address—followed by a comma;
3. a body of at least one paragraph, with paragraphs indented about five spaces;
4. a complimentary close (roughly aligned with the return address) two or more lines below the last paragraph; the close varies: *Love, Much love, Cordially, Affectionately, Best always, As ever.*
5. your signature (nickname, first name, or full name, depending on the relationship) just below the closing.

MODEL FOR PERSONAL LETTERS

375 High Street
San Carlos, CA 94070
July 21, 1980

Dear Aunt Gladys,

We got home yesterday, and my body is still protesting. Too little sleep, too much food, and too many miles by car and plane. Still, what joy to see all of you after so many years.

I should thank you again for making our stay in Topeka the highlight of our trip. Thanks for finding — and paying for — such beautiful rooms at the Holiday Inn and for the gracious dinner you served Friday evening. Thanks also for introducing us to so many friends and neighbors (which reminds me —

please thank Wally for letting me use his drill).

I'll have to give you the details in a longer letter. I just wanted to tell you that Arkansas was all I expected. We did get to see the cemetary and the old bank building in Viola. Then we drove to Rodney, which has almost disappeared. It's true there's a farm and a church nearby, but of the town itself only the post office remains, and that's closed and abandoned; its windows broken, its foundation crumbling, it's bent over like an old man walking into the wind. Daddy said, "_This isn't Rodney._" But of course it was — and now I have the faded post office sign to probe it. I took several rolls of pictures, and I _promise_ to send you copies as soon as I can get them processed.

Love and best wishes to Aunt Wilma.

Love,
Martha

MODEL FOR ADDRESSING PERSONAL ENVELOPES

Martha St. John
375 High Street
San Carlos, CA 94070

Mrs. Gladys B. Williams
1978 Oak Street
Topeka, KS 66606

Although the size varies, the envelope for personal letters
is addressed in roughly the same way as the envelope for
business letters: the writer's name and return address are
neatly written in the top left-hand corner; the name and
address of the person you're writing to are centered
(approximately).

Glossary of Grammatical Terms

Grammar describes words and how they fit together to form the basic unit of our language, the sentence. It may, of course, be perfectly true that you learned to speak English or another language grammatically not by learning the rules of grammar but by imitating the people around you. It is equally true, however, that until you learn these rules or conventions you cannot see or explain how language works. Once you know the rules you can figure out when and why something is wrong in your speech or writing and how to correct it. The following explanations, then, all deal with words and how they fit together to form sentences.

active voice Active voice is the form of the verb used when a subject performs the action: "Claire *runs* the show." See also **passive voice** and pages 91, 149–150, 182.

adjective One of the eight parts of speech, an adjective describes or modifies a noun or pronoun. Most adjectives answer

All terms printed in color appear as separate entries in this glossary.

those old familiar questions—which one, what kind, how many: green cheese, German beer, some pretzels. See also pages 5–8.

adverb   One of the eight parts of speech, an adverb describes or modifies a verb, adjective, or another adverb: "Seeing the *frighteningly* realistic mask, Martha screamed *very shrilly.*" *Frighteningly* describes the adjective *realistic; shrilly* describes the verb *screamed; very* describes the adverb *shrilly.* See also pages 9–10.

agreement   Agreement is the consistency in number (singular or plural) between subjects and their verbs and between pronouns and their antecedents: "*Joel goes* to art class to improve *his* painting. *Joel and Marie go* to the movies to see *their* favorite actors." In the first sentence, the singular verb *goes* agrees with the singular subject *Joel* and the singular pronoun *his* agrees with its antecedent *Joel.* In the second sentence, the plural verb *go* agrees with the plural subject *Joel and Marie* and the plural pronoun *their* agrees with its antecedent *Joel and Marie.* See also pages 11–18.

antecedent   An antecedent is the noun to which a pronoun refers: "*Kit* took *his* barbells to *Gwen's* house for *her.*" *Kit* is the antecedent of the pronoun *his* and *Gwen* is the antecedent of the pronoun *her.* See also pages 11–13.

appositive   An appositive is a word or phrase that appears next to and explains a noun: "Wilbur, *the man in the dusty-rose jumpsuit,* is the campus boxing champion." Use commas around appositives except when they are very short and there is no appreciable pause before them: "The designer *Givenchy* inspired Wilbur's jumpsuit."

article (determiner)   *A, an,* and *the* make up one of the eight parts of speech called articles or determiners. These three words function as adjectives: "Hugo ran *a* mile, drank *an* eggnog, and hit *the* floor."

auxiliary verb   An auxiliary, or helping, verb—usually a form of *to be* or *to do*—is used with a main verb to show a change in time, number, mood, or voice: "I *was* studying this morning, I *am* studying now, and I *will* study tonight because I *do* want to pass Dr. Freud's exam."

case   Case is the form nouns and pronouns take to indicate their function in a sentence. In English, both nouns and pronouns take the *possessive, or genitive, case.* Pronouns also take the *subjective, or nominative, case* if they function as the subject of a verb or a subject complement and the *objective case* if they function as the object or indirect object of a verb or as the object of a preposition: "*We* (subjective) brought *them* (objective) the pizza (objective), but *Jack's* (possessive) friends took *it* (objective) for *themselves* (objective)." See also pages 30–35.

clause   A clause is a group of related words containing a subject and a verb. See **dependent clause** and **independent clause.**

collective noun   A collective noun is a word that is singular in form but that indicates a group that may be either singular or plural: "The *cast was* assembled on the stage." (Here the singular verb indicates that *cast* is considered a single unit.) "The *cast were* in different parts of the theater." (In this sentence the plural verb shows that *cast* means all the separate individuals.) Other common collective nouns include *team, faculty, herd, committee.*

comparison   Comparison is a change in the form of adjectives and most adverbs to show quantities or qualities. There are three degrees of comparison: ***positive*** (fine, good, softly), ***comparative*** (finer, better, more softly), and ***superlative*** (finest, best, most softly). Note that some words change completely in comparison: good, better, best; you must learn these individually. However, add er or est to most one and two syllable adjectives: kind, kinder, kindest. Add more or most to adjectives of three or more syllables and most adverbs: meaningful, more meaningful, most meaningful; quietly, more quietly, most quietly.

When comparing two people or things, use the comparative degree: "Ingrid is *thinner* than Amy." When comparing three or more people or things, use the superlative degree: "Rocky claims that his mother is the *sweetest* person who ever lived." See also page 146.

compound sentence   A compound sentence is a sentence that is made up of at least two independent clauses: "The winners went to the bank, and the losers went to the poorhouse." "Jackie became a well-known editor; Pat remained the gay divorcée." See also pages 42–43.

conjunction   One of the eight parts of speech, a conjunction is a word that joins other words or word groups. The two types of conjunctions are ***coordinating*** and ***subordinating.*** Coordinating conjunctions join items that are of equal importance in a sentence. In English there are only six coordinating conjunctions: and, but, or, nor, for, yet. Subordinating conjunctions join a dependent clause and an independent clause. Here are just a few of the many subordinating conjunctions: as, because, before, if, since, until, when. See also pages 42 and 84.

conjunctive adverb   A conjunctive adverb is a word or phrase that functions as a connective between independent clauses. As an adverb, it shows *logical*—but not grammatical—relationships between such clauses. Technically, the conjunctive adverb is said to modify the verb in the independent clause to which it belongs, but some grammarians consider such connectives as "whole-sentence modifiers." In either case, conjunctive adverbs perform an important function in writing by showing relationships as you move from one sentence—or from one paragraph—to another. Among the more common conjunctive adverbs are *and, consequently, first, second* (*third*, etc.), *however, in any case, therefore,* and *finally*. See also pages 209–211.

correlatives   Correlatives are coordinating conjunctions that function with other words in pairs: both . . . and, either . . . or, neither . . . nor, not only . . . but also, whether . . . or. See also page 140.

demonstrative pronoun   A demonstrative pronoun is a pronoun that distinctly points out something. There are four demonstrative pronouns: this, that, these, and those.

dependent clause   A dependent, or subordinate, clause is a clause that contains a subject and verb but cannot stand alone. It can function as an adjective: "The voting booth *that Jerry selected* was at the end of the row." It can function as an adverb: "*When I become president,* you will see some major changes." Or, it can function as a noun: "I said *that I would do it.*"

determiner   A determiner is a word that indicates that a noun follows. Determiners include the articles *a, an,* and *the,* as well as such other markers as *my, your, her,* and *these.*

direct object   A direct object is a word that receives the action of an active transitive verb. It answers the question what or whom: "He fulfilled his campaign *promise,* and he appointed *her.*"

ellipsis   See pages 80–81.

expletive   Since Watergate, many people think of an expletive only as an obscene word or phrase. However, in the grammatical sense, an expletive is a "filler" word that takes the place of the subject of a sentence when that subject follows the predicate. The words *there* and *it* are expletives: "*There* were fewer than three million ballots cast in my state" as opposed to "Fewer than three million ballots were cast in my state." Avoid expletives unless doing so would result in an awkward-sounding sentence.

finite verb   A finite verb is the principal verb of a clause or sentence. All verbs are finite except infinitives, participles, and gerunds.

function words   Function words have no meaning in themselves, but they show relationships among other words and indicate how these other words function. Among the function words are articles, determiners, conjunctions, and prepositions: "*The* host *and* guests all remembered *that* party *in the* park."

gerund   A gerund is a verb form that ends in *ing* and functions as a noun. Like other nouns, a gerund can function as a subject ("*Jogging* is not my idea of a good time"); a complement ("My pet peeve is *jogging*"); or an object ("Finally, he gave up his *jogging*").

imperative mood   See **mood.**

independent clause   An independent, or main, clause is a word group containing a subject and a predicate that can stand alone as a simple sentence: "The die is cast."

indicative mood   See **mood.**

indirect object   An indirect object is a noun or pronoun to or for whom or to or for what something is done. An indirect object usually comes before a direct object: "Carly gave *roller skating* a bad name." When the indirect object is a pronoun, use the objective case: "Carly gave *me* a shove." If the preposition *to* or *for* is used, the words which follow become the object of the preposition, not an indirect object: "She gave the shove to *me*."

infinitive   An infinitive is a verb form consisting of the word *to* and the present form of the verb itself. An infinitive can function as a noun ("*To err* is human"); an adjective ("Janie has songs *to sing*"); or an adverb ("Guido fights *to get* attention").

inflection   Inflection is a change in the form of a word or its ending to show a distinct meaning. The most frequent inflections occur in verb endings (come, comes, coming, came); noun endings (tree, trees, tree's); pronoun changes (*I, me, my, mine*) and comparison endings of adjectives and adverbs (grand, grand*er*, grand*est*; grand, grand*ly*).

interjection   One of the eight parts of speech, an interjection is a word used to show violent emotion and in writing is usually followed by an exclamation point (Ah! Nuts! Wow!).

intransitive verb   An intransitive verb is a verb that does not need an object to complete its meaning: "The water boils." Many verbs may be either transitive or intransitive depending on how they are used: "Judy *ran* this morning" (intransitive). "Judy *ran* the projector" (transitive). See also pages 6–8.

linking verb   A linking verb is a verb that joins, or links, the subject and complement of a sentence; it does not show action or require an object. The most commonly used linking verb is *to be*: "Sebastian *is* my friend." Other common linking verbs include *to seem, to become, to look.* Still other linking verbs, such as *to feel, to hear, to smell, to taste,* may also be used as nonlinking, or transitive, verbs: "The air *smells* wonderful" (linking). "I *smell* a rat" (nonlinking, or transitive). See also pages 6–8.

modifier   A modifier is an adjective or adverb that describes or otherwise specifies a particular noun or pronoun. For example, "an apple" is extremely general and could indicate any apple on earth. "A green apple" is more specific, ruling out all red and yellow apples, for instance. However, "that tiny green apple sitting on the right-hand corner of Joe's desk" is about as specific as we can get. Note that modifiers may be single words, phrases, or clauses.

mood   Mood is the form of a verb that shows whether the verb is expressing a fact or asking a question; expressing a condition contrary to fact, a desire or wish, or doubtfulness; or expressing a command. Use the ***indicative mood*** to state a fact or ask a question: "She *kissed* him soundly." Use the ***subjunctive mood***

for a condition contrary to fact, a wish, or a doubt: "If I *were* she, I would not have kissed him so soundly." Use the ***imperative mood*** for a command: "*Stop* kissing him this instant."

nonrestrictive clause   See **restrictive and nonrestrictive clauses.**

noun   One of the eight parts of speech, a noun names a person, place, or thing. ***Common nouns*** name a general person, place, or thing (man, city, newspaper). ***Proper nouns*** name a particular person, place, or thing (John D. Rockefeller, Los Angeles, *The New York Times*). Note that proper nouns are capitalized while common nouns are not.

Nouns may serve a number of functions in a sentence.

Subject: "*Stars* shine."

Direct object: "Rockefeller handed out *dimes.*"

Indirect object: "Rockefeller gave *people* dimes."

Object of the preposition: Rockefeller gave them dimes outside the *church.*"

Complement: "Rockefeller was a *philanthropist.*"

object   An object is a noun or pronoun that falls into one of three categories. A ***direct object*** receives the action of a verb and answers the question what or whom. An ***indirect object*** tells to or for whom or to or for what something is done. An ***object of a preposition*** follows a preposition and is the last word in a prepositional phrase.

participle   A participle is a verb form that usually functions as an adjective or part of a verb phrase: "The *drowning* man was *saved.*" Participles have three tenses. The present participle ends in *ing*: "*Heralding* his arrival, the band played 'Hail to the Chief.'" The past participle usually ends in *d* or *ed*, *n* or *en*: "*Taken* with her beauty, Lem fell in love." The past perfect participle takes the auxiliary verb *being* or *having*: "*Having* run twelve miles, they dropped from exhaustion."

parts of speech   Language experts traditionally classify words into eight categories on the basis of their form, meaning, use, and position in a sentence. These eight categories, or parts of speech, are nouns, pronouns, verbs, adjectives, adverbs, conjunctions, prepositions, and interjections. Each of these is dealt with in this glossary.

passive voice   The passive voice is the form of the verb used when a subject is acted upon: "The projector was run by Judy." See also **active voice** and pages 91, 149–150, 182.

phrase   A phrase is a group of related words that does not contain a subject and predicate. Among the most frequently used phrases are noun, verb, and prepositional phrases. "*The elegant old gentleman* tipped his hat" (noun phrase). "He *has seemed tired* since he returned from the hospital" (verb phrase). "Once more, dear fellow, *into the breach*" (prepositional phrase).

possessive   The possessive is the form, or case, of a noun or pronoun that shows ownership. Possessive nouns take 's or s' endings or are preceded by the preposition *of*: "Sissy's photograph exactly matched the description *of Medusa*." Pronouns have their own individual possessive forms. See **pronoun.**

predicate   A predicate is one of two basic parts of the sentence—the other being the subject—and says something about the subject. The main part of the predicate is the verb, which is sometimes referred to as the ***simple predicate.*** A ***complete predicate*** includes the verb and all its modifiers. "Martha St. John joined the French Foreign Legion last October." (*Joined* is the simple predicate; *joined the French Foreign Legion last October* is the complete predicate.)

preposition   One of the eight parts of speech, a preposition is a word that shows the relationship of its object to some other word or words in the sentence. Among the many words that often function as prepositions are these: about, above, across, after, among, at, before, behind, below, between, beyond, by, down, for, from, in, into, near, of, off, on, over, through, to, toward, under, until, upon, with, and without.

pronoun   One of the eight parts of speech, a pronoun is a word that takes the place of a noun—its antecedent. In most instances, the pronoun refers to the noun that comes just before it: "If *Steve* gets *his* way, *he* and *Jenny* will take *her* car to school tomorrow." Here are the five most commonly used types of pronouns.

Personal pronouns agree with their antecedents in person, number, gender, and case.

	Subject		Object		Possessive	
	Singular	Plural	Singular	Plural	Singular	Plural
1st Person	I	we	me	us	my	our
2nd Person	you	you	you	you	your	your
3rd Person	she, he, it	they	her, his, its	them	hers, his, its	their, theirs

These *demonstrative pronouns* point to something specific: this, that, these, those.

These *interrogative pronouns* answer a question: who (whom, whose), which, what.

These *indefinite pronouns* refer to general or unnamed antecedents: anybody, anyone, each, everybody, everyone, somebody, someone (used with singular verbs); all, none, some (used with singular or plural verbs according to context).

These *reflexive pronouns* refer back to the subject: myself, yourself, herself, himself, itself, themselves. (The same pronouns used immediately after the subject are called *intensive pronouns*, as in "I myself will do it.")

See also pages 11–13, 30–35.

restrictive and nonrestrictive clauses   A restrictive clause is essential to the meaning of the main clause. A restrictive clause is not set off by commas: "The book *that has given me the most trouble* is the one you are reading now." A nonrestrictive clause is not essential to the main clause and may be omitted without changing the basic meaning of the sentence: "This book, *which was lost for over one hundred years*, is the most handsomely illustrated volume I have ever seen."

sentence   A sentence, the basic unit of our language, is a word or group of words that can stand alone and sound complete: "Go!" "I will leave now." Sentences usually have a subject, which is most often a noun or pronoun about which something is being said, and a predicate, which always contains a verb and is what is said about the subject: "Izzy laughed." (In this sentence, *Izzy* is the subject and *laughed* is the predicate.)

There are a number of ways to classify sentences. Let's look at three of them.

Depending on their **purpose,** sentences may be classified into four types.

    1. *Declarative sentences* make a statement that gives the reader or listener some kind of information: "This is boring, so I am going to bed."

    2. *Interrogative sentences* ask a question: "Do you mind if I go to bed?"

    3. *Imperative sentences* give an order or request something: "Please turn out the light before you go to bed."

4. **Exclamatory sentences** state a strong feeling: "What a pain you are!"

By using these four types of sentences, you will get different kinds of responses from your reader or listener.

Depending on their **structure,** sentences may be classified into four different types.

1. **Simple sentences** contain one main, or independent, clause made up of a subject and predicate: "Evan slammed the door."

2. **Complex sentences** contain one main clause and at least one subordinate, or dependent, clause: "Evan slammed the door, although no one was around to hear him."

3. **Compound sentences** contain at least two main clauses: "Evan slammed the door, and the dishes rattled in the cupboard."

4. **Compound–complex sentences** contain at least two main clauses and at least one subordinate clause: "Evan slammed the door, and the dishes rattled in the cupboard until some of them shattered."

By combining these different types of sentence structures, you can add variety and rhythm to your writing.

A third way of classifying sentences is according to the arrangement of their components, or their **patterns.** In English, we have five basic sentence patterns.

1. **Subject–verb:** "Money *talks.*"

2. **Subject–verb–object:** "Money sometimes *brings happiness.*"

3. **Subject–verb–indirect object–object:** "Money *brought her happiness.*"

4. **Subject–verb–subject complement:** "Money *is a powerful tool.*"

5.   *Subject–verb–object–object complement:* "The bank elected Martha its first treasurer."

See also pages 177–182.

simple sentence   See **sentence.**

subject   A subject, usually a noun or pronoun, is the part of a sentence about which something is said: "*Edith* often burns their dinner."

subjunctive mood   See **mood.**

subordination   See pages 195–196.

superlative   See **comparison.**

tense   Tense is a verb form that indicates time. See also **verb** and pages 183–184, 197–198.

transitive verb   A transitive verb is a verb that needs an object to complete its meaning: "Oscar dried the baby." (*Baby* is the object of the transitive verb *dried.*) See also pages 7–8.

verb   One of the eight parts of speech, a verb indicates action or a state or being. A verb is the basic component of the predicate of a sentence.

As stated elsewhere in the glossary, *transitive verbs* require an object to complete their meaning: "The attendant demanded cash." *Intransitive verbs* do not require an object to complete their meaning: "Luci blinked." Some verbs can be transitive ("Harold called his mother") or intransitive ("Harold called loudly"). A *linking verb* is an intransitive verb that joins a subject and its complement: "Rasputin is my friend."

Verbs indicate time through the use of *tense.* By themselves English verbs can show only two tenses: present and past. With the help of auxiliary verbs, however, we can show six tenses:

Present	He cheers.
Past	He cheered.
Future	He will cheer.
Present Perfect	He has cheered.

Past Perfect	He had cheered.
Future Perfect	He will have cheered.

Voice—either active or passive—is a quality of transitive verbs. The passive voice is achieved by adding a form of *to be* to the past participle of the main verb.

ACTIVE	PASSIVE
She runs the show.	The show is run by her.
She ran the show.	The show was run by her.
She will run the show.	The show will be run by her.

Note how the direct object (*show*) in the active-voice sentences becomes the subject in the passive-voice sentences.

See also **mood, finite verb, infinitive, verbals,** and pages 6–8, 13–18, 149–150, 183, 197–198.

verbal   A verbal is a word made from a verb but used as a noun, adjective, or adverb: "*Skiing* is hard on the ankles" (*Skiing*—a gerund—is used as a noun and is the subject of this sentence). "I felt a *sinking* sensation in the pit of my stomach" (here *sinking*—a participle—is used as an adjective to modify the noun *sensation*). "Rachel sat on the floor *to catch her breath*" (in this sentence, *to catch* (her breath)—an infinitive—is used as an adverb to modify the verb *sat*). See also **gerund, infinitive, participle.**

voice   See **active voice, passive voice, verb,** and pages 91, 149–150.

Glossary of Usage

This glossary discusses in brief a generous selection of the words and constructions that may confuse students who use this handbook. We have attempted to be useful and practical instead of exhaustive, since the scope of our little handbook is necessarily restricted to the most troublesome writing problems confronting college students.

It is important to note that only General English, a variety of Standard English, can be recommended as appropriate to most college writing. See the main entry on **Usage** for a more detailed outline of the characteristics of Standard and Nonstandard English. For convenience we will define the following terms here:

1. *Standard English:* the spoken and written language of educated men and women; comprising General English, Informal English, and Formal English.

2. *Nonstandard English:* the language of illiterate people, of certain dialect groups, and of some minorities.

3.   *Informal English:* the language used by educated people in private conversations, personal letters, and writing intended to be close to popular speech; a variety of Standard English.

4.   *General English:* the spoken and written language of the educated majority; essentially a literary language used in business letters, book reviews, student essays and examinations, professional fiction and nonfiction of all sorts, and an extensive variety of other writing. The vocabulary of General English consists largely of those words *not* marked by usage labels in dictionaries.

5.   *Formal English:* essentially a written language, characterized by a precise, extensive vocabulary, with a high proportion of words derived from Latin and Greek; appropriate to technical, scientific, and academic writing; less occasionally appropriate to student writing (the Formal vocabulary and construction often seem wooden, stilted, and pretentious, especially in the prose of beginning writers).

6.   *Colloquial:* belonging to the constructions and idioms of conversation and informal writing; not appropriate to most college writing; definitely not appropriate to formal writing.

7.   *Slang:* "the body of words and expressions frequently used by or intelligible to a rather large portion of the general American public, but not accepted as good, formal usage by the majority" (Stuart Berg Flexner, *Dictionary of American Slang*). Under most circumstances, slang is not acceptable in college writing.

In preparing this glossary of usage we have consulted the following reference works: *Webster's Third New International Dictionary, Webster's New World Dictionary of the American Language* (Second Edition), *The American Heritage Dictionary of the English Language, A Dictionary of Contemporary American Usage* by Bergen Evans and Cornelia Evans, *Dictionary of American Slang* by Harold Wentworth and Stuart Berg Flexner, and *The Oxford English Dictionary*.

A, an.   Use *a* before words beginning with a consonant or a sounded *h: a book, a lighter, a pair, a hotel.* Use *an* before words beginning with a vowel or vowel sound: *an ant, an hour, an orange.*

Accept, except.   Do not confuse. *Accept* is always a verb meaning "to take or receive": "I accepted Donna's gift with pleasure." *Except* may be either a verb or a preposition. As a verb it means "to exclude": "The instructor excepted only a few students from the exam." As a preposition *except* means "leaving out": "Everyone was happy except Fred."

Ad.   Colloquial shortening of *advertisement.* Prefer the full word.

Affect, effect.   Do not confuse. Most commonly *affect* means "to influence": "Your grade will be affected by class participation." *Effect*, as a verb, means "to cause to happen; to bring about": "The medicine effected the desired result." *Effect* is also a noun meaning "result": "The effect of stress on the production of hormones is now being studied by medical researchers."

Ain't.   Nonstandard (often dialectal) contraction of *am not, are not, has not, have not.* Sometimes used for shock value in educated speech. Do not use in college writing.

Alibi.   Colloquial for *excuse.* Standard only in the legal sense of "the plea or fact that an accused person was elsewhere than at the alleged scene of the offense with which he is charged."

All right, alright. The correct spelling is *all right. Alright* is Nonstandard—and is almost always considered a misspelling.

Alot.   Misspelling of *a lot. Alot* occurs with amazing frequency. Avoid!

Alternate, alternative.   Distinguish between these two words. *Alternate* usually means every other one, while *alternative* indicates choice, or one of two choices: "They had no alternative but to arrange that each one would take the car to work on alternate days."

Among, between.   *Among* always indicates more than two: "There was real friendship among members of that English class." *Between* generally designates only two ("Between Jim and me there is enough money for bread and cheese") but may be used, according to the *Oxford English Dictionary*, "to express the relation of a thing to many surrounding things severally and individually," as in "a treaty between three powers."

Amount, number.   Use *amount* to express quantity, bulk, or mass, *number* to refer to countable items: "a large amount of flour" but "a number of apples."

And etc.   Redundant: *etc.* is an abbreviation of the Latin phrase *et cetera*, "and other [things]." *Et* MEANS "and."

Anxious, eager.   Although these two words are often used interchangeably and some dictionaries even list them as synonyms, many language purists insist on maintaining a distinction between them. *Anxious* means "uncertain or troubled" (note the relationship to *anxiety*), while *eager* means "impatiently desirous." "Because Nick thought he had done well on the exam, he was eager to know his grade. Jessie, on the other hand, felt she had done poorly and was anxious about her grade."

Anyways.   Dialectal (Nonstandard) for *anyway* or *in any case:* "I may not do well in French, but I try anyway."

As.   Overused and imprecise when substituted for *because* or *since* to introduce a clause. Prefer "I didn't work in the garden because I was tired" to "I didn't work in the garden as I was tired."

As to.   Wordy. Prefer *about:* "I don't know about that date, but I'll check my calendar."

Awful, awfully.   *Awful,* in the sense of "very bad," is colloquial. "The food was awful" might be acceptable under some circumstances, but "The food was abominable" would generally be preferred. *Awfully,* meaning "extremely" or "very," as in "I was awfully excited," is also colloquial.

Bad, badly.   *Bad* is an adjective, *badly* an adverb: use *bad* after a linking verb ("I feel bad tonight") and *badly* with action verbs ("Cohn behaved badly when he beat Pedro Romero"). *Badly* in the sense of "very much" is colloquial: "Jake needed Brett very much (not *badly*)."

Being as.   Nonstandard for *since, because.* Do *not* write "Being as I was very hungry, I ordered a dozen oysters, a seafood salad, the assorted shellfish platter, a bottle of Blue Nun, cheesecake, and a pot of coffee." Begin "Since (or *because*) I was very hungry. . . ."

Beside, besides. *Beside* means "by the side of": "I sat beside Martha St. John." *Besides* means "in addition to": "Besides me, there were Jonathan Wild, Martha St. John, and Gilmore Stern."

Between. See **Among, between.**

Broke. Colloquial in the sense of "without money."

Bunch. Colloquial in the sense of "group" or "gathering," as in "a bunch of people."

Bust, busted, bursted. Nonstandard forms of *burst*; present and past tenses and the past participle are all spelled *burst*.

Can, may. *Can* means "be able to"; *may* means "have permission to": "Lisa can sing well." "May I sing tonight?" *Can* in the sense of "have permission" is colloquial.

Can't hardly. Nonstandard (dialectal): a double negative. Use *can hardly*.

Complected. Colloquial or dialectal for *complexioned*. Prefer the latter.

Considerable. An adjective: "I spent a considerable amount of money last month." Do not use as an adverb, as in "I like her considerable."

Contact. Many people sensitive to language object to using *contact* as a verb. Prefer *arrange to meet, consult, talk with,* or even (if you must) *make contact with.*

Continual, continuous. Distinguish between these two words. *Continual* means "occurring repeatedly; going on in rapid succession": "Laura's continual interruptions annoyed Professor Thrumbottom." *Continuous* means "extending without interruption in either space or time": "We can measure but not really feel the continuous movement of the earth around the sun."

Contractions.   Though slightly informal, contractions such as *won't*, *can't*, and *haven't* are usually acceptable in General English despite objections from purists and conservatives. Contractions are not appropriate, of course, in highly formal writing.

Could of.   Nonstandard for *could have*.

Data.   Plural of *datum*, which is almost never used. *Data* is often treated as a singular, however, as in "This data is misleading."

Definitely.   Often objected to as imprecise and overused in the sense of "positively, certainly": "I'm certainly (not *definitely*) going to visit my hometown next summer."

Different than.   Now considered colloquial. Prefer *different from*, as in "I am an individual, different from every other person who has ever lived."

Disinterested, uninterested.   *Disinterested* means "impartial" or "unbiased": "Did they find a disinterested person who could referee the game objectively?" *Uninterested* means "not interested": "Because Judy was uninterested in the final score, she left the game early." Although some dictionaries have come to accept *disinterested* as a synonym for *uninterested*, many English teachers insist that the distinction be maintained for the sake of precision.

Due to.   Do not use in the sense of *because of* or *owing to*; there is strong and not entirely unreasonable prejudice against such use: "Because of (not *due to*) the long day in the sun, my cat Mephisto seemed quite contented with life." There is no objection to the use of *due* as an adjective: "My check is due soon."

Effect.   See **Affect, effect.**

Either, neither.   Designates one of two (not one of more than two): "Either of these [two] dictionaries is satisfactory" but "Not one of these [three] books is appropriate."

Emigrate, immigrate.   *Emigrate* means "to leave one country or region to settle in another." *Immigrate* means "to come into a new country in order to settle there."

Enthuse.   A colloquial substitute for "be enthusiastic." Avoid such usages as "My friends are enthused about my role in *Ten*."

Etc.   Abbreviation of the Latin phrase *et cetera*, "and other [things]." Do not use *etc.* carelessly or loosely; instead, make a real effort to develop your ideas with effective details. See **And etc.**

Expect.   Colloquial in the sense of "suppose" or "suspect."

Farther, further.   Generally, *farther* is used to express distance and *further* to mean "in addition; more." "The ball went farther than I thought it would" but "Further discussion of your grade is pointless."

Faze.   A colloquial verb meaning "to disturb, disconcert." Do not confuse *faze* with the noun *phase.*

Fewer, less.   *Fewer* is used with numbers, *less* with degree, value, or amount. "Fewer than thirty people attended the game." "Our dinner at Spenger's cost less than we thought it would." Note: the sign at the supermarket checkout counter should read: "EXPRESS LANE—FEWER (not *less*) THAN EIGHT ITEMS." Combat imprecise language.

Fix.   Most commonly means "to make firm, stable, or secure." Dialectal or colloquial in the sense of "prepare, intend," as in "I'm fixing to do my homework."

Funny.   Colloquial for *strange, odd, queer.*

Guy.   Colloquial for *boy* or *man*. Used carelessly, imprecisely, and far too frequently. Do not use this word in college writing.

Hang.   An object is *hung*; a person is *hanged* (executed). The principal parts are *hang, hung, hung* (object) and *hang, hanged, hanged* (person).

Hisself.   Nonstandard for *himself*.

Hopefully.   Use this adverb only when you mean "with hope": "The natives waved hopefully as the handsome young president drove past." Just as you would not use *carefully* to mean "I care" or "it is cared," do not use *hopefully* to mean "I hope" or "it is hoped," as in "Hopefully, I'll sleep tonight."

Imply, infer.   *To imply* is "to suggest": "The instructor implied that his students didn't write well." *To infer* is "to draw a conclusion": "The students inferred that their instructor was dissatisfied with their writing."

In, into.   *In* means "located within": "I was standing in the room." *Into* denotes "motion to a point within": "Sam walked into the room."

Infer.   See **Imply, infer.**

Irregardless.   Nonstandard for *regardless*.

Its, it's.   *Its* is the possessive pronoun. *It's* is the contraction of *it is*. Do not confuse these words: to do so is inexcusable.

Just.   Colloquial when used in the sense of *simply* or *completely*, as in "I was just [simply] teasing."

Kind of, sort of.   Colloquial for *somewhat, rather*: "The children were kind of [rather] excited about their trip to Bear Valley."

Lay, lie.   In the most common uses, *lay* is a transitive verb meaning "set, place." *Lie* is an intransitive verb meaning "recline." Transitive verbs take direct objects; intransitive verbs do not.)

The principal parts of *lay* are

lay (present tense), as in "Lay the book on the desk";

laid (past tense), as in "Margo laid the book on the desk";

laid (past participle), as "The concrete was laid yesterday."

The principal parts of *lie* are

lie (present tense), as in "Lie down";

lay (past tense), as in "I lay down for an hour";

lain (past participle), as in "I have lain here for an hour."

Lay and *lie* are not particularly difficult words for those who take the time to learn the differences between them and who care enough about language to want to use it precisely and correctly. We urge you to learn—and to care.

Lend.   See **Loan, lend.**

Less.   See **Fewer, less.**

Lie.   See **Lay, lie.**

Like, as, as if.   In General English observe the following distinctions:

Like (preposition): "She dresses like a mature, sophisticated woman."

As (conjunction): "Do as (not *like*) I say."

As if (conjunction): "This book looks as if (not *like*) it might make difficult reading."

In short, do not use *like* as a conjunction: it is colloquial; it wears the taint of commercial jargon; and there is strong prejudice against it, especially in slightly more formal shades of General English.

Literally.   *Literally* means "actually" or "without exaggeration." Never use this word (He was literally green with envy) when you mean its opposite, *figuratively*.

Loan, lend.   Although these two words are sometimes used interchangeably in General English, prefer the distinction between the noun *loan* and the verb *lend*: "If you lend him your charge plate, you may regret the loan for the rest of your life."

Lose, loose.   Different in meaning and pronunciation. *Lose* means "to fail to keep." *Loose* as a verb means "to unbind, set free"; as an adjective, "free, unbound."

Lots, lots of.   Colloquial for *many, much, a great deal of*: "Mr. Warburton makes a great deal of (not *lots of*) money."

Mad.   Colloquial for *enraged, angry, furious*, although recorded in these senses as early as 1300 (*Oxford English Dictionary*). In Formal English *mad* means "insane."

May.   See **Can, may.**

May of.   Nonstandard for *may have*.

Mean.   Colloquial for *bad-tempered, disagreeable, malicious*.

Might of.   Nonstandard for *might have*.

Mighty.   Colloquial in the sense of *very*, as in "I'm mighty pleased to meet you."

Most.   In the sense of *nearly*, a colloquial form of *almost*. General English: "We visit Yosemite almost (not *most*) every summer."

Must of.   Nonstandard for *must have*.

Neither.   See **Either, neither.**

No place.   Informal for *nowhere*.

Number, amount.   See **Amount, number.**

Of.   Nonstandard for *have* in such constructions as *could have, might have*.

Off of.   Formerly in standard use but now dialectal. "I fell off
(not *off of*) the balcony."

OK, O.K., okay.   Colloquial for *satisfactory, all right, correct.*

Ought to of.   Nonstandard for *ought to have.*

Out loud.   Frequently considered colloquial. Prefer *aloud* in
more formal writing.

Per.   Correctly used in *per pound, per foot*, etc. *As per* is
redundant—and tainted by commercial use. Avoid "as per
instructions" and similar phrases.

Phone.   Considered colloquial. Use *telephone* in more formal
writing.

Photo.   Colloquial form of *photograph*. Use the full word in
more formal writing.

Plenty.   Informal when used as an adverb.
Informal: "The redwoods are plenty tall."
General: "The redwoods are certainly tall."

Prefer.   Usually followed by *to:* "I prefer this to that." Do not
follow by *than*, as in "I prefer steak than seafood."

Pretty.   Generally accepted for *moderately, fairly,* or *somewhat,*
but weakened by overuse. Vary it by judiciously chosen
synonyms.

Principal, principle.   Do not confuse. *Principal* as an adjective
means "chief, main, first in rank or authority"; as a noun,
"governing or presiding officer." *Principle*, a noun, means
"ultimate source; fundamental truth or law."

Prof.   Slang when used as common noun in place of *professor*,
as in "The prof mutters in a low, monotonous voice." The best
practice is to write the word in full on all occasions: "Professor
Jones is a brilliant lecturer."

Quiet, quite. *Quiet* is an adjective meaning "motionless, hushed." *Quite* is an adverb meaning "completely, entirely." Do not confuse.

Raise, rise. *Raise* is a transitive verb; its principal parts are *raise, raised, raised:* "I have raised frangipanis for many years." *Rise* is an intransitive verb; its principal parts are *rise, rose, risen:* "I rise early on school mornings." "The sun rose at 6:13 A.M." "I had risen at 5:00 A.M. in order to write a lecture for my eight o'clock class."

Real. Colloquial as an intensive adverb meaning *really* or *very,* as in "The steak was real good."

Reason is because. General English requires *reason is that.* Colloquial: "The reason you don't sleep well is because you don't get enough exercise."
General English: "The reason you don't sleep well is that you don't get enough exercise."

Reckon. Dialectal or colloquial for *believe, suppose, think,* as in "I reckon I'll do it if I want."

Right. As an intensive adverb meaning *very,* colloquial or dialectal (Southern U.S.): "He's a right smart boy." Prefer *very* in General English.

Set, sit. Often confused. The principal parts of *set,* meaning "to place," are
set (present tense), as in "I now set the cup on the table";
set (past tense), as in "I set the cup on the table";
set (past participle), as in "I had set the cup on the table."
Set is perfectly clear, straightforward, and regular, but it is often confused with *sit. Sit* is usually an intransitive verb; its principal parts are
sit (present tense), as in "I now sit down";

sat (past tense), as in "I sat down";
sat (past participle), as in "I have sat [not *set*] down."
As noted, mistakes generally occur in the use of *set* for *sit*. Do not write "I am setting down." "Set down, friend," or "I set down to do my homework." All such usages are incorrect.

Should of.   Nonstandard for *should have*.

Show up.   Colloquial when used to mean "be superior to," as in "Our team showed up the Cougars."

So.   Overused as a coordinating conjunction, as in "It was a sunny day, so we went to the beach." Try to achieve variety by substituting conjunctive adverbs for *so-* constructions: "Writing is hard work; consequently, I seldom write for more than four hours at a time." You can also make other changes in sentence structure: "It was such a sunny day that we went to the beach."

Some.   Informal when used for *a little* or *somewhat*, as in "I rested some yesterday." Slang when used as an intensive. "He is some (meaning *superior*) student."

Sort of.   See **Kind of, sort of.**

Such.   Colloquial for *to a great degree*, as in "He is such a good teacher." This and similar constructions are careless and vague.

Swell.   Slang for *very good, excellent*, as in "We ate at a swell French restaurant."

Terrible.   Colloquial for *very bad*.

That there.   Nonstandard for *that*: "That (not *that there*) song brings back sad memories."

Their, there, they're.   Do not make an exhibit of your ignorance or carelessness by confusing these words. *Their* is a possessive pronoun, *there* an adverb, and *they're* the contraction for *they are*.

This here.   Nonstandard for *this*.

Thusly.   Pretentious. Prefer the simple form *thus*.

To, too, two.   Do not confuse the preposition *to* ("to the cabin") with the adverb *too* ("too much to eat") or the numeral *two* ("two steaks"). Do not use *too* in the sense of *very*, as in "I am not too fond of him."

Unique.   Means "one of its kind." Hence logically something cannot be "very unique" or "more unique." Although the informal senses of the word ("remarkable, uncommon") are clear enough, it is best to avoid them in General to Formal English.

Used to could.   Nonstandard for *used to be able* (*could* does not have an infinitive form).

Wait on.   Colloquial or dialectal when used to mean "wait for."

Ways.   Informal for *distance*, as in "We have come quite a ways."

Where.   Informal in such a sentence as "I read where almost no jobs are available for teachers." The accepted construction uses *that*: "I read that almost no jobs are available for teachers."

Where . . . at.   Informal and redundant, as in "Do you know where Jon's at?" Prefer "Do you know where Jon is?"

Where . . . to.   Informal and redundant, as in "Where are you going to?" Omit the *to*.

Which, who.   Do not use *which* to refer to people: "Lisa is a girl who (not *which*) can sing and dance like a professional."

While.   Overused as a conjunction when *and* or *but* would serve better. *While* most precisely designates time: "I wrote while my father read."

Would of.   Nonstandard for *would have*.

You all.   Dialectal for *you* (Southern U.S.). Prefer *you* in General English.

INDEX

All important terms, rules, and concepts in the text of the handbook are indexed here. The reader should note, however, that the index does not *directly* cover material presented in the Glossary of Usage and the Glossary of Grammatical Terms, although occasional duplication occurs. *Gerund*, for instance, is indexed, but it is also defined in the Glossary of Grammatical Terms, which supplements definitions given in passing in the text. Both the index and the glossaries are indispensable to the student who seeks to use the handbook with minimal confusion and maximum benefit.